To my long-suffering parents,
my charming sisters and
my soul-mate, Tim.

DEAR LUPIN

Charlie and Roger Mortimer

Constable • London

Constable & Robinson Ltd
55–56 Russell Square
London WC1B 4HP
www.constablerobinson.com

First published in the UK by Constable,
an imprint of Constable & Robinson Ltd, 2012

Published in this paperback edition by Constable, 2013

A copy of the British Library Cataloguing in
Publication data is available from the British Library

ISBN: 978-1-78033-235-2

Printed and bound in the UK

1 3 5 7 9 10 8 6 4 2

Roger Mortimer was born in 1909 and educated at Ludgrove, Eton and Sandhurst. In 1930 he was commissioned into the Coldstream Guards. He fought in Dunkirk in 1940 and was taken as a POW for the remainder of the war. After resigning from the army in 1947, he became a racing correspondent for the *Sunday Times* for almost thirty years. He wrote several classic books on racing including *The History of the Derby*. He met Cynthia Denison-Pender in 1947 and was married the same year. They had two daughters: Jane and Louise and one son, Charles. He died in 1991.

Charlie Mortimer was educated at Wellesley House and (reluctantly) Eton. Now describing himself as a 'middle-aged, middle-class spiv (mostly retired)', he was, amongst other things, in the Coldstream Guards, a vintage car restorer, oil-rig rough-neck and pop-group manager, as well as a boat boy in Kenya, car salesman in California, scrap-metal dealer, manufacturer of boxer shorts and antiques dealer. He lives with his partner in West London.

'[The letters] are among the funniest ever dispatched in the vain hope of steering a black sheep on to something like the straight and narrow.'
Frederic Raphael, *Wall Street Journal*

'Wry, trenchant, often extremely funny, but also charmingly forbearing and forgiving.'
Rupert Uloth, *Country Life*

'Entirely delightful: funny, wise and full of insights into the relationship between fathers and sons.'
Carolyn Hart, *The Lady*

'This is by far the funniest book I've read this year... It's also extremely touching.'
Evening Standard Books of the Year

'Not to be read where helpless laughter, or tears, may embarrass the reader.' Brian Sewell

'Hilarious...witty and affectionate.... Letter writing may be a dying art, but this book proves what a glorious art it is.'
Sebastian Shakespeare, *Tatler*

'These delightfully funny missives from an eccentric father to his errant son have all the playful oddity of the Dear Bill letters.' Roland White, *Sunday Times*

'As well as being the funniest book I've read in ages, it's also extremely touching. A delight then, on every front.'
John Preston, *Spectator*

Preface –
A Tribute to Mr Pooter

This book is a tribute to my dad and a big thank you to him for never giving up on me despite my endless shortcomings, failures, disasters and general inability to live up to the high hopes and aspirations he and my mother had for me, which, as these letters show, over time became slightly more realistic. Initially there were hopes that I would get my house colours at Eton and become an officer in the Coldstream Guards. Ultimately my dad merely hoped that I would avoid 'being taken away in a Black Maria' together with my then business associates, the now infamous John Hobbs (the colourful Chelsea antiques dealer to the mega-wealthy) and his brother Carlton. However, it is now twenty years since my dad died and I suspect he would be delighted that, now almost sixty, the same age he was when he wrote me the early letters, I had at least survived thus far and was moderately happy.

As he predicted it is only in later life that I have come to fully appreciate the affection and wisdom imparted by him to me. I am grateful that, despite what he described as my 'unorthodox lifestyle', I somehow managed to keep the majority of the letters he sent me, which is somewhat of an achievement in itself. At an early age I was aware that they were something special and not at all like the letters that my friends' fathers sent to them. In fact, I used to regularly read them out loud, often after a few drinks, to whomever I was with at the time and there were always many laughs, mainly at my expense.

My dad was enormously self-deprecating. He saw himself as a patiently enduring and thoroughly respectable middle-class gentleman, much along the lines of Mr Pooter in *The Diary of a Nobody*, while I was the disreputable son, Lupin, who was always getting into frightful scrapes. Thus many of the letters start 'My Dear Lupin' before launching into a thoroughly bleak assessment of my current situation and future prospects. The early letters were largely of concern and admonishment but, as time went by, a resigned accept-ance of the way things were crept in. Despite everything, my father never showed me anything other than affection and tolerance.

I think in later years he almost used writing as a form of therapy to deal with his own ups and downs and this, together with his unique and sometimes devastating perspective on almost anything, made the letters real gems that have clearly stood the test of time. He was a great pricker of ego, self-importance and pomposity.

He was also a total original, as indeed was my dear mother, thus his descriptions and analogies of people, situations and such are both a breath of fresh air and highly entertaining. I clearly remember him summing up Yoko Ono, when she first came on the scene, as being 'as erotic as a sack of dead ferrets', while in one of his *Sunday Times* articles (*c*.1971), he wrote, 'At one time a little humdrum adultery could prove a barrier to The Royal Enclosure at Ascot but now something more spectacular is required, such as hijacking a Securicor van or taking too prominent role in a sex education film designed for circulation in the best preparatory schools.'

This little collection of literary snapshots in the form of letters is a celebration both of a long-suffering father's enduring relationship with his ne'er-do-well son and a humorous insight into the life of a mildly dysfunctional English middle-class family in the 1960s, 1970s and 1980s.

A Bit of History

My dad was born Roger Francis Mortimer on 22 November 1909. My grandparents were pretty well off and lived in a house in Cadogan Gardens, Chelsea, London. According to the 1911 census there were eight 'live-in' staff members. My grandfather, Haliburton Stanley Mortimer, was a charming man but by all accounts not a great stockbroker. My grandmother, Dorothy (née Blackwell) was an heiress of the well-known food company Crosse & Blackwell. My father had one sibling, Joan, born in 1907.

He was educated at Ludgrove School, Eton College and Sandhurst. In 1930 he was commissioned into the Coldstream Guards. He was a captain when his platoon fought a desperate rear guard action at Dunkirk in 1940 during which almost all of his men were killed and he was wounded. Unconscious, he was taken prisoner and spent the remainder of the war in prison camps running the camp radio. Many of my father's friends in later life were those he met as prisoner-of-war no. 481 in various Oflags and Stalags.

After the war he rejoined his regiment and, as a major, served in Trieste. However, in 1947 he resigned and took up an appointment with Raceform, the official form book for horse racing. He followed this by becoming racing correspondent of the *Sunday Times* until retiring almost thirty years later. He also wrote for various other newspapers, was a commentator for the BBC and became PR officer to the Tote. In addition, he wrote several classic books on racing, the greatest of which was undoubtedly *The History of the Derby*. His other books on racing included *The Jockey Club*, *Anthony Mildmay*, *Twenty Great Horses* and *The Flat*. My dad was also a keen gardener and quite an expert on military history.

He met my mother, Cynthia Denison-Pender, in 1947 and within six weeks had proposed to her. They were married in St Paul's, Knightsbridge, on 10 December of the same year. My older sister Jane was born in 1949, myself in 1952 and my younger sister Louise in 1957.

Dramatis Personae

Family

My mother: Cynthia Sydney Mortimer aka Nidnod (née Denison-Pender, born 28 February 1921).

My older sister: Jane Clare Torday aka Miss Cod-Cutlet, Miss Cod's Eyes, Miss Fisheyes, Miss Bossy Pants (née Mortimer, born 23 January 1949).

My younger sister: Louise Star Carew aka LL, Lumpy Lou (née Mortimer, born 12 January 1957).

My brothers-in-law: Paul Torday (married older sister, 1971; two sons, Piers and Nick); Henry Carew aka HHH, Hot Hand Henry (married younger sister, 1977; one daughter, Rebecca, and one son, Benjamin).

Father's mother: Dorothy Mortimer aka Gar (née Blackwell).

Father's sister: Joan Cockburn (née Mortimer, born 1907; married to Reggie Cockburn aka Uncle Reggie).

Mother's sisters: Pamela Darling aka Aunt Pam (née Denison-Pender, born 1913; married to Kenneth Darling aka

General Sir Kenneth Darling); Barbara Fellowes (née Denison-Pender) aka Aunt Boo (born 1915; divorced).

Father's first cousins: Tom Blackwell; John Blackwell (my godfather).

Father's first cousins once removed: Tom Blackwell's son, Charlie, and daughter, Caroline.

Father's aunts: Shirley Blackwell (née Lawson-Johnson); Margery Blackwell (never married).

Mother's aunt: Phyllis Shedden aka Aunt Pips (née Fisher; married Norman Loder, then Lindsay Shedden).

Pets

Turpin (wonderful black mongrel); Moppet (the cat); Pongo (Dalmation); Soloman aka Tiny Man, Solly, Cringer (fox terrier); Peregrine aka Perry (chihuahua); Baron von Otto aka The Baron, Otto (chihuahua).

Gardeners

Mr Randall aka Randy; Keith Bailey.

Domestics

Jenny and Audrey.

Neighbours

Colin and Sarah Bomer, and their two sons, Mark and William; the Roper-Caldbecks; Farmer Luckes; Lord Carnarvon; the Adams boys.

Dad's 'prisoner-of-war friends'

John Surtees aka Mr S. (and wife Anne); Desmond Parkinson

aka Mr P. (and wives Heather, then Paddy); Freddy Burnaby-Atkins (and wife Jenny); Fitz Fletcher (my godfather); Francis Reed; Sir Frederick Corfield QC aka Dungy Fred.

Dad's horse-racing friends

Nick and Judy Gaselee; John and Liz Pope; Peter Willett; John and Jean Hislop; the Cottrills; Dick Hern; Peter Walwyn; the Wallis family.

Other family friends

Agnete Cameron aka Mrs Cameron (my godmother); Gerald and Helen de Mauley aka Lady de Mauley; Nancy and Richard McLaren; Rodney Carrott; Raoul and Sheelagh Lemprière-Robin; the Hambros; Joyce Walker; the Grissells; the Tollers; the Yarrows; Paul Majendie; the Thistlethwaytes; the Guinness family (bankers); the Edgedales.

My school tutors

Norman Addison aka CNCA (House Tutor); John Faulkner aka Ordinary Faulkner (Classical Tutor); Michael Kidson (Modern Tutor).

My friends

Probably the less said about them the better but including: Pete Breitmeyer aka Peter Carew; George Rodney; Jeremy Soames; Charlie Hurt aka Chicken Hurt, Le Poulet; Charlie Shearer; Joe Gibbs; Andrew Brudenell-Bruce; Tony Simmons aka Tony S.; Robin Grant-Sturgis; Charlie Higgins; Mollie Salisbury aka Lady Salisbury, the Marchioness of Salisbury; James Staples.

Other characters and acquaintances

Simon Sandbach; the Greenwells; Jeffrey Bernard.

Family homes

Barclay House, Yateley (1950–67); Budds Farm, Burghclere (1967–84); The Miller's House, Kintbury (1984–2006)

It all started for me on Grand National Day, 1952.

My dad's job was that of racing journalist and radio commentator and he was up in Liverpool for the big race at Aintree. The following observations were written at the time in my blue 'Baby Book' by my mother: 'Charles Roger Henry kept us waiting three weeks to the day and then arrived at his home Barclay House at five minutes to eight on the morning of Friday April 4th. Jeanie his nurse (and mine!) only rang the doctor at 7.15 so he was literally scrubbing up in technical terms when Charles shot himself into the world. It was quite thrilling to hear I had a lovely son and see him on the bed beside me. The moment I had been revived by a cup of tea I rang up Roger at Liverpool and caught him still in his room. I knew he would never believe he really had a son. Charles himself was the happiest of babies, so placid and easy.'

Roll on fifteen years and it's a rather different story . . .

1967

The Sunday Times
3 February

Dear Charles,

I hope all goes well with you. I never seem to hear of you unless some disaster, major or minor, has taken place. Owing to lack of communication on your part, I have not the remotest idea of what is going on at Eton or how you are progressing, if at all, in your work. Jane has not come down this weekend and I have no idea what she is up to. Nor do I know where she is living: she might be on the run from the police judging from the rapidity with which she changes her domicile. I had a bad and painful attack of gout last week and now I have a throat infection and am partially deaf. Getting old is revolting and I hate it. Poor David Gundry, who stayed at Barclay House a couple of times, was killed in a car accident last week. He went off the road at 90 mph and that was that. A tragic waste of a young life. We are now off to lunch with the Hislops. Last week we went to the theatre and saw 'The Secretary Bird, which is very light but by no means unamusing. Inspector Barlow and the man who plays his boss were sitting just behind us. I had to drive to Doncaster and back last week which was rather tiring. Louise is home and seems in good form. She is the one member of this family that gives me no trouble.

Best love,

D

I am now fifteen years old and enjoying a somewhat undistinguished career at Eton College. In an end-of-term report, my Classical Tutor sums up the situation thus: 'Nero was content to roll in the dust in order to collect his laurels. Mortimer however seems merely content just to roll in the dust.'

Budds Farm
23 May

Dear Charles,

It was nice to hear from you again after rather a long interval! I'm glad to hear that life seems to be going reasonably well. What has happened to Ordinary Faulkner to make him so cheerful? The prospect of getting rid of you, I suppose! I am going over to Eton if I can tomorrow for Charles Gladstone's Memorial Service. I woke up this morning with the house stinking of oil and full of smoke. One of the boilers had gone all wrong and a chimney was on fire, too. I switched the boiler off, opened the windows and went to bed. I saw a hideous car pile-up on Saturday. Two cars – a Zephyr and a Cresta – were upside down and one had gone over a ditch and into a field. Two people were killed. Louise and Jane come home tomorrow. Thank God it is slightly warmer today. I have had a couple of barmy letters from Gar. One of Mr Luckes's cows got loose in the garden and was a great nuisance. Are you keen on pictures by Toulouse-Lautrec? If you are I will send you a book on him. I think in future I shall call you 'Lupin' after Mr Pooter's son in 'The Diary of a Nobody'. I'm sure Mr Kidson would agree it is very suitable for you.

Yours ever,
D

And so I take on the name of Lupin, the disreputable son who was the source of much of Mr Pooter's worries.

1968

Budds Farm
28 January

Dear Charles,

Your mother came back rather sad and depressed after seeing you yesterday. You may think it mildly amusing to be caught poaching in Windsor Great Park; I would consider it more hilarious if you were not living on the knife edge, so to speak. I know there is always a temptation for boys who fail to make their mark at work or games to try and gain a reputation as a law-breaker and a defier of authority. I trust you will not give way to that particular temptation. If you do, judging from your past record of folly, you will end up with the sack from Eton or with gaol. Doubtless you regard me as a monumental bore, tolerated at times only because I fork out some cash, but senile as I am I probably know a bit more about you and your friends than you seem to realise; and what I know, I do not necessarily like. As you are so clearly reluctant to discuss your future with me, I have written to Mr Addison to ask for his advice on that point. I have suggested you are wasting your time at Eton. I shall also ask whether in his opinion you are sensible enough to be allowed at large in Paris with Soames. I hate writing to you like this but I do care so much for you and it is distressing for me and your mother to see you making such a hash of your opportunities. No doubt you resent my advice and reproaches now; perhaps in ten years' time you will realise that I was trying, possibly ineffectively, to help you. I'm not God and my advice is not necessarily right, but as I care for you I must do what I can within the limits of human error. At least you have parents that love you; some people do not even have that consolation.

    D

I am quite happy with my little escapades although nobody else is. 'The knife edge' referred to is the fact that I am on a final warning following a flogging from the headmaster as punishment for visiting a certain 'Denise Bunny' in London one night. A couple of appearances in Maidenhead magistrates court for riding a 750 cc Ariel motorcycle without a driving licence or any other paperwork haven't really helped much either.

The Sunday Times
12 March

My Dear Charles,

    I am writing to you in confidence so please do not discuss this letter with anyone. That silly young ass Simon Sandbach has got himself into a real muddle and is now in a mental hospital, where he will remain for at least six months. I think he has been drinking and sampling drugs, too. It is really very sad. I have known people do very stupid things at Eton with regard to drink, sex, gambling and, more recently, drugs. I implore you not to experiment even in the mildest way with drugs. Probably you have not the slightest intention of doing so, but it is quite easy to be tempted by others who may regard the experiment as harmless which of course it is not. I think on the whole you have plenty of common sense but as you grow older you may tend to find life at Eton tedious and restrictive; if you do, don't commit some act of folly that could have dire consequences for yourself. It would be much better if you left and did a job of work if you honestly felt that Eton was no longer of any benefit to you and that you were no longer of any benefit to Eton. Perhaps this letter is unnecessary, but it is a worry to me when a boy like S. S. suddenly goes right round the twist. It is all too easy to go off the rails at Eton and once off it is not simple to get back on again. I rely on your common sense to keep within the bounds of decorum!!

Yours ever,

D

Any letter starting 'My Dear Charles' is generally well worth avoiding. This particular letter contains much excellent advice, all of which goes totally unheeded.

1969

Budds Farm
16 January

Dear Charles,

I assume you got back safely last night. Time is running short so do try and get through this half without disaster and without a chorus of disapproval and despair from the unfortunate masters who have to try and teach you something. Unless Mr Addison and Mr Kidson can provide strong arguments to the contrary, I propose that you leave Eton at the end of the summer. After all, you are not interested in work or games and you have no ambition to assume responsibility in your House or in the school as a whole, so what would be the point of staying on? I suggest that on leaving you either go into the Army for three years or alternatively I will give you a single ticket to Australia and £50 and you go and earn your living there for a couple of years. I think you need to stand on your own feet and not rely on the efforts of others. Before you go into business, you must learn a little about life so that you have something to offer an employer. I have just had a letter from Aunt Joan asking me whether you received a Christmas present from her as she has received no acknowledgment. As in other matters of life, you are childishly idle about writing letters, thereby giving the impression that you are both ill-mannered and ungrateful. If people can bother to give you a present, the least they can expect is that you rouse yourself from your customary state of squalid inertia and write and say thank you. It was disgraceful that you were still writing thank-you letters on the last day of the holidays. Surely you can see for yourself that your idleness and refusal to do any little task that is in the slightest degree irksome renders you totally unfit for adult employment? I am very fond of you but you do drive me round the bend.

D

Dad is getting rather stressed out. The idea of joining the Army or going to Australia for a couple of years is not really what I have in mind.

Budds Farm
26 February

Dear Charles,

We really must formulate some plans for the future. Various questions have got to be settled.

1. Will you leave at the end of the Summer Half or would it help you to stay on?
2. If you leave, where are you going in September? A definite plan is essential. I am not keen on crammers as most of the pupils are undisciplined louts who have failed to make the grade at school.
3. Is it important for you to have A levels? If so, are you more likely to obtain them by staying at Eton or by having tuition elsewhere? By elsewhere, I do not mean London or any other place where there is not strict supervision.
4. What is your objective to be? What are you aiming for? What qualifications do you require?

Perhaps you could discuss these matters with your Modern Tutor?

Not much news. Old General Scobie died from a heart attack. He stopped Greece going communist in 1945. Your mother has had flu. Her little plan to give up spirits for lent lasted 3½ days. Pongo has chewed up a rug and had very bad diarrhoea in the kitchen. Six Indians were killed in a car crash in Newbury.

Best love,

D

Unfortunately for Dad making plans is not on my list of priorities unless it involves the procurement of fairly large quantities of mind-altering substances. Obtaining qualifications is of scant interest.

The Sunday Times
2 March

My Dear Charles,

Thank you for your letter. Very well then, you can leave Eton at the end of the Summer Half. Make the best use of the little time that is left to you there and don't do anything stupid. Perhaps I ought to have realised much earlier that you are not really suitable material for Eton and that a smaller school would have suited you better. I cannot pretend that your career there has been anything but a bitter disappointment to me and at times a source of profound anxiety. Both your House Tutor and your Modern Tutor agree that you ought to leave as you seem to have no future as a specialist.

The next problem is to find something for you to do and a place for you to go when you leave. I have a poor opinion of crammers. The pupils tend to be boys who have failed to make the grade morally or intellectually at school and the same can all too often be said of those who teach there. There is some truth in the old saying that there is no cad to equal a crammer's cad. Your Modern Tutor holds an even lower opinion of crammers than I do and is well aware of the type of conduct so often rife at those institutions. Great care, therefore, must be taken to find a place which will not encourage your tendency to play the part of the little lawbreaker. In particular I do not wish you to go to the same place as one or two of your less responsible Eton friends. Your Modern Tutor has asked me to go and see him and with his help no doubt something can be worked out. I think you must realise you have come to a crossroads in your life. If you elect to take the wrong road

12

now, the consequences could be very grave indeed. As you grow older, people are less willing to laugh off delinquency.

I am all in favour of you getting a couple of A levels but what worries me is that in ten years of costly education, you have never had a good report and have never got down to hard work. What assurance have I got that you will work harder and be more responsible away from school? Plenty of boys seem to get A levels at Eton without working themselves into a state of collapse. Why not you?

You can rely on me to do all I can to help you but you can hardly blame me for being cautious, even sceptical, after some of the incidents of the past year. Our family all tend to be late developers and I think you come into that category, too. I think you have it in you to lead a useful and happy life but very soon you must take yourself by the scruff of your neck, shake yourself and determine to get down to work and be less self-indulgent.

Jane is here and sends her love. She is going to France at Easter with some people I have never heard of. Louise has a ghastly cough and Solly has picked up an infection and is thoroughly unwell. A girl was stabbed in Yateley outside Janice's home. The Camberley Art Centre in Camberley High Street has been burnt down; arson is suspected. I saw one of your nicer friends, Higgins, at Kempton. Mr Parkinson is showing signs of marrying again. I hope it will be third time lucky.

Yours ever,

D

P.S. Never forget that your mother and I love you very much and perhaps that is why we worry so much and I feel compelled to write long and probably pompous letters of admonition and reproof. We both long to see you happy and settled, and whatever mistakes we make over you, they are made with the best possible intentions.

Clearly my time at Eton has been a disaster all round. Despite my poor parents' supremely good intentions I am not the ideal candidate for England's premier public school.

Budds Farm
22 March

Dear Charles,

I enclose £12 for leaving presents. Please deduct 10/ and have your hair cut. As by the end of the week you will no longer be a school boy, there is no necessity for you to look the part any longer.

Naturally I am distressed at you leaving Eton so suddenly and with so little accomplished, but you have evidently been determined to leave and of course you have got your way. What next? I simply don't know. Most unfortunately – and perhaps this is my fault – you cannot communicate your thoughts, fears and hopes to me, and in all but the most trivial matters we are strangers. Because of this I cannot help you as I should like. Something seems to have gone very wrong somewhere, but I am almost entirely in the dark. I think, and those who know you best at Eton agree, that you have been unfortunate in the past year in your choice of friends.

Naturally I am worried about you, desperately worried, possibly because I know so little of the true situation. Perhaps we can sort something out when you come home but you will need to be franker and more communicative than in the past. Possibly I am less unsympathetic than I appear on the surface; my own adolescence was beset with problems and I made many mistakes. I cannot direct your life; at the most I can guide, advise and perhaps help in a few small ways but to carry out those functions I must have a little help from you.

I suppose the process of growing up is difficult, confusing and sometimes painful for you; it brings sometimes grief and worry to parents, too. I feel very sad when I think of the fun we used to have in the old days. Perhaps something can be salvaged from the wreck before the gulf between us gets impossibly wide.

I wonder if you realise how lucky you have been in the last year in having a House Tutor and a Modern Tutor who both like you, have always been at pains to emphasise to me your best points and always speak up for you. When you are older, you may realise you owe them a considerable debt.

Best love,

D

Largely oblivious to the distress and disappointment of my folks I simply cannot wait to leave. The term after I depart, a boy in my house is caught smoking. When the housemaster punishes him he objects: 'That's not fair, sir. You allowed Mortimer to smoke.' 'Now,' says my old House Tutor with suitable gravitas, 'there was a boy who really needed to smoke.'

I enclose for your attention my telephone bill (Jumbo size). Please note calls to Hurt at 8/0, 11/4 and 18/. I think no further comment is needed but please be temperate in this matter. I don't think I overcharged you!!

D

29 May

Thank you for your card, you cheeky monkey! I hope you are settling in and that the crammer is not too hopeless!

The Gaselees are staying here tonight and a man of eighty-four with a beard comes to lunch tomorrow. I am off to the Derby Dinner tonight + visit General Fisher en route. Nidnod is in a flap and keeps losing £5 notes; I think she is under the impression that I pinch them. I have paid for your shares – Woodfall Trust – keep an eye on them. I'll get you the receipt, don't lose it, it is very important as regards tax. Some men are putting down carpet in the W.C.

We had a disgusting dinner in Newbury last night.

Be reasonably good,

D

I am now lodging in Brighton with Joyce Walker, a friend of my parents. She has a wonderful voice crafted over the years from generous quantities of untipped Virginia cigarettes and Gordon's gin. I attend a crammer daily in the vain hope of finally reaching the heady heights of knowledge required to bag a humble Maths O level.

The Sunday Times
4 June

My Dear Lupin,

I am glad to hear you are happy at Brighton and that all goes reasonably well. I don't suppose you will want to come home at the end of the month! There were two communications for you today from the Ministry of Defence and I opened them just in case they were urgent and knowing they would not be personal. One says you have been accepted for the Regiment (as a candidate); the other is about your five days at Tidworth starting on 13 July. I want you to be at the Old Coldstreamers party here on 13 July and you can drive to Tidworth (only thirty miles) in my car or Nidnod's afterwards. Incidentally it was Fred who drew the ticket (Belbury) in the Sweep.

Yesterday I had to go to a memorial service for Brigadier Cazenove, who commanded the 1st Bn in Belgium in 1940. Quite a nice service and I am always very moved when the band plays old Coldstream marches at the end of the service. It was pouring with rain when I came out but luckily I got a lift with Major Pope.

In the afternoon I went to 'Oh What a Lovely War'. Of course I enjoyed the songs, but it not a film for me as firstly I remember the first war quite well; secondly I was a soldier for seventeen years; and thirdly I have studied military history.

I have seen many of the people portrayed in the film and of course the actors bore as much resemblance in appearance and character as Mick Jagger does to Alice in Wonderland. In the entire film there was not one single person who looked like a soldier; they looked like actors – some of them not very good ones – in clothes hired from a seedy provincial theatrical costumier. History was twisted to give a certain point of view, and it was so far from the truth that I was seldom moved at all. I thought a ghastly tragedy was too often turned into rather tawdry farce. I cannot read the official history of the Battle of the Somme without tears coming into my eyes at the thought of the flower of English manhood being slaughtered – most of them not conscripts or regular soldiers but young and idealistic volunteers. I was tremendously moved by World War I in that BBC serial because it showed the terrible truth and did not distort facts to produce rather naive and bogus propaganda. If our leaders had been all such dolts, how in God's name did we win against the might of the greatest military power the world has ever known, backed by the superb planning and organisation of the German General Staff? At the start of that war we could put about seven divisions (12,000 men in each) into the field; the Germans about 130. Haig was admittedly stubborn, unimaginative and insensitive, but he won in 1918 some of the greatest victories ever achieved by British arms. The film, with cheap and puerile inaccuracy, seems to try and make out that all officers were nits and took no part in the fighting; in fact casualties among officers were proportionately far higher than among other ranks as they had to lead and take more risks. Look at the names on the 1914–18 war memorial at Eton. In most regiments, relationships between officers and other ranks in war-time are very close, based on shared risks and inter-dependence for survival.

In the evening I went to Whitehall to hear the massed bands

of the Guards Division, with the mounted bands of the Household Cavalry, beat retreat. I think you would have enjoyed some of it, particularly the introduction to 'Lohengrin' and one or two slow marches; possibly, too, 'Chitty Bang Bang' and the 'Posthorn Gallop'!

Some more pictures come up for sale at Christie's on 20 June. I saw the solicitor about your inheritance yesterday. It will be invested at compound interest till you are twenty-one when you can do as you please. Jane will get hers right away.

Give my love to Joyce.

D

In a moment of madness I agree to go on a trial five-day stay with the Coldstream Guards. Unfortunately in the interim I am arrested for possession of drugs and a flick knife at the Rolling Stones concert in Hyde Park, which rather puts the damper on things. This letter arrives just prior to all the drama. My mother is particularly annoyed that I appear on the front page of the Newbury Weekly News, overshadowing the mention on the back page that her Dalmation, Pongo, had taken first prize in the fancy-dress class as the Captain of HMS Pinafore.

I have just paid a telephone bill for the enormous sum of £68. As I have hardly used the telephone at all myself, I shall be grateful for contributions.

RM

Another phone bill and Dad pleads poverty.

Budds Farm
Sunday

Dear Charles,

I am very impulsive. Your mother is also very impulsive. That is quite enough for one family. Let us have a little planning, forethought and sensible deliberation from you. So to start with, get rid of that bloody bicycle. I did not give you £40 for that, as you well know!

Yours ever,
RM

The 'bicycle' alluded to is actually my motorcycle, a beloved Honda Monkey Bike.

Dear Charles,

As a bourgeois reactionary, I am inclined to think you pursue your code of being scruffy and uncouth a little too far. Last night you parked the Bubbler flush with the front door so that elderly guests arriving for dinner could hardly get in the house at all. Dinner was at 8.15 and you saw fit to appear at 8.40, well after the guests. Even allowing for the fact that you cannot yet tie a bow tie, a sweat rag coiled round your neck is a somewhat unattractive form of evening dress. Your hands looked as if you had been greasing a No. 19 bus and had given them a quick flick over with a damp sponge. When called to the telephone, you saw fit to stay away for fifteen minutes; hardly a compliment to your neighbours at the dinner table.

I don't expect you to be a second Lord Chesterfield, but I rather wish that in appearance and conduct, you were slightly less typical of a transport cafe on the Great North Road.

Don't get into trouble tonight!

D

An absolute classic. 'The Bubbler' is my purple bubble car with faux tiger-skin seat covers.

1970

With regard to your trip to Greece, I wish to make the following points, which no doubt will be totally disregarded:

1. Make sure before you start that your passport is in order + that you have the required visas for yourself and documents for your car. It is important to carry full insurance.
2. Drive carefully. In Europe they are far, far tougher on motorists than they are here. If you get involved in an accident, you may easily and up in gaol. It would be quite beyond my power to extract you if, for instance, you get locked up in Yugoslavia.
3. On no account get involved in any form of political argument. The Greeks love politics and arguments and Greece is now a Police State.
4. Have nothing to do with drugs unless you are particularly keen to pass the next seven years in prison.
5. Try not to look like some filthy student who has renounced

personal hygiene completely. The unwashed with long hair are looked upon with great hostility in certain European countries and it would be silly to be stopped at a frontier because you like wearing your hair like a 1923 typist.

6. If you do get into trouble, Interpol will soon find out you have a police record and that could be awkward.

7. Take plenty of money. You need not spend it all.

8. Take a small medicine box and plenty of bromo. You are one of nature's diarrhoea sufferers.

9. Make sure all your headlights are adapted to the rules of the country you are in.

10. If in trouble, contact the British Consul.

11. Some of the drink in Greece is very powerful indeed and can give you the most appalling headache.

12. Be v. careful to whom you give a lift. Stick to girls, they are safer and usually more amusing.

13. Do not carry a flick knife or any nonsense of that sort.

14. Take a shady hat; the temperature in Greece will be over 100°F and sunstroke is rather unpleasant and distressing.

15. Enjoy yourself + don't do anything too stupid. I trust you + P.B. together not quite as far as I could kick a thirty-ton concrete block.

RM

Time for my summer holiday. This is a final fling before rather an impetuous decision to join the Coldstream Guards as a squaddie in October. Due to a conviction for possession of marijuana I am not able to join as a potential officer. As the Colonel in Chief remarks to me in an interview, 'If you were merely an alcoholic we wouldn't give a damn.'

7 October

My Dearest Charles,

I am very clumsy at having little talks with my own family so I will try, no doubt inadequately, to say a few things before you leave to join the Coldstream. Firstly, I wish you every possible good fortune and happiness. I was never a particularly good soldier but I was a very happy one. It would be untrue to say, though, that I was happy straightaway; I was not. I had anxious, even unhappy days before I settled in. I have no doubt that in the next few weeks moments, perhaps days, will occur when you will curse your decision to join; you will feel tired, frustrated, angry and totally fed up. I certainly went through that phase during my first term at Sandhurst and I wondered if I was ever going to make the grade; I did, but it was a near thing once or twice. You have two assets; firstly, in a stoical sort of way you have plenty of courage; secondly, you have a sense of the ridiculous, a sense without which the Army is hardly the ideal profession for civilised individuals. I think you get on with people, too. Also you are good with your hands whereas I was, and am, inconceivably inept. Your fellow recruits will probably be working-class boys from the north. Most of them will have never left home before and you will in many ways be tougher and more worldly-wise than they are. Also you are – or at least ought to be – rather better educated. So you will have certain advantages. From the start play by the rules even if you think the rules are silly; show yourself above all reliable and a trier; don't, above all, try any smart tricks or chance your arm in any way; you will come off second best. Just try your hardest

24

even at truly ghastly things like PT which I myself hated above all. Be very clean at all times; Army doctors have a nasty little trick of making inspections and examining every inch, literally, of your anatomy and if they find anything not 100 per cent clean they send in an adverse report. Keep your money locked up; don't lend any and watch your kit. I don't think you will have any serious troubles but if you think there is anything seriously wrong – bullying or petty dishonesty by older soldiers or NCOs – let me know at once. That sort of thing is rare, very rare in the Coldstream, but it is not absolutely impossible. When you get allowed out of barracks, watch your step very carefully and don't do anything silly. If anything, be a bit of a prig to start with!

That is really about all, and quite enough too. Remember I am here in the background to help all I can if anything goes wrong. Don't hesitate to ring me up or write. I will always do what I can. That is what fathers are for.

Your affectionate father,
RM

10 October

Dearest Nidnod and dearest Jane,

I am writing you a joint letter about your son/brother (cross out the description that is inapplicable). If I seem a bit off beam, it is because I have a nasty go of salmon trout and am as stuffed with drugs as a sucking pig is of sage and onions – though through a different aperture. On

Wednesday I tried to help Charlie get ready for Pirbright and gave him an inadequate parting gift of forty cigarettes, some nail scissors and a box of band-aid. In the evening the Bomers came to dinner and Sarah gave Charles a present and a big kiss. The dinner was daintily served by Mr Gracious Living (me) and the chicken cooked with mushrooms and the unexpended portion of yesterday's vin rouge was delicious. Charlie was in excellent form after three champagne cocktails and gave us some hilarious and slightly hair-raising stories of his experiences and misadventures with Boris and Co. He really is a cheeky monkey! Thursday was a perfect autumn day and we set off from Pirbright at 10.30 a.m. leaving Jenny holding back the tears as if Charlie was off to Vietnam. Charlie drove the Rover and we went through Blackdown where my old father joined the Army – in 1914 at the mature age of thirty-five. At Pirbright we stopped 100 yards from the entrance and Charlie, tense, pale and utterly stoical – shades of Wellesley House – entered the guardroom, case in hand. I waved farewell and drove on to Brookwood to get some petrol. I then drove back and going through Pirbright I saw a lone figure, suitcase in hand, walking with that well-known rolling gait across a gigantic and otherwise empty barrack square. I felt it was perhaps symbolic of a gentle, indolent and rather impulsive boy entering a rather tough, demanding world of men. It reminded me of the famous final shot in one of Charlie Chaplin's long films – was it 'The Kid'? I couldn't help thinking of so many episodes from Charlie's boyhood – the happier ones for the most part like picnics at the Robbers Cave, family holidays, opening presents at Hartletts on

Christmas day and so forth. It is the greatest possible error at my time of life, when the brain is beginning to soften, to lapse into drooling sentimentality, a lapse caused in this case by the over-protectiveness felt by parents towards their children. At all events, once in the mood I could not get out of it. On my way to Ascot I dropped in at the Wallis's house and left a wedding present for Nona. Then on through Camberley where I pictured Jane and Charles at the station waiting for my father's train; on up the hideous High Street with memories of you and I doing hectic last-minute shopping for the children's stockings. I drove through the RMAS grounds where forty-two years previously, on a similar autumn day, I had arrived bewildered and far from happy. It was here you bowled to a coloured gentleman in the nets, where we took Turpin for walks, and where I marched you up a steep hill to expedite the arrival of Louise. I suddenly remembered my old instructor Captain Hancock who painted insipid watercolours. He asked me to tea at his bungalow, 'Kashmir Lodge', and showed me his painting of the trees round the lake at Sandhurst in October. It bore the title 'Leaf by golden leaf crumbles the gorgeous year'; poorish art and indifferent poetry, but the fact that I recollect it after forty-two years confers on Captain Hancock, dead these many years, a form of immortality. Then on through Yateley, past old dear Barclay House and up Mill Lane where we had family walks with Jane rather 'bolo', Charles in a pushchair and scarlet hat and Turpin sniffing for unattractive objects in the ditches. I seemed to see a shade of the late Mr Townroe striding briskly along with his walking stick and nosy-parker expression. Up past the Gunns' house and then to W. H. Smiths where an owlish lady with unfortunate dentures once conducted the lending library. At this point nostalgia had turned to nausea so I entered a pub next door to where the Wellington Hotel once stood and ordered a stiff drink which broke the spell and gave me violent hiccups. Charlie starts off at £14 a week of which he can draw £5, the rest being saved on his behalf. His address is C. R. H. Mortimer, Coldstream Guards, Guards Depot, Pirbright, Surrey. I shall make no effort to see him just yet as I want him to settle down. If he can get a day off, he can take a train from Brookwood to Basingstoke and be met there. All being well, he will be home for Christmas.

xx R

These two letters really sum up what a tremendous man my dad was. Who could ask for more than this from a father?

Budds Farm
14 October

Dear Charles,

I have just had a call from Tony S. so will tear up and disregard your letter. Give the Army a chance. You simply must not think of quitting after five days. You say the life is unpleasing to you and will do you no good; I assure you that to bail out after a few days would damage your reputation among all who know you beyond repair, and would do you far more harm than a recruits' training course! I implore you to grit your teeth and stick it. If, after twelve weeks, you are still convinced that you are totally unsuited to the Army, then that is a different matter. But to concede defeat now is unthinkable.

Yours,

D

Life in the Brigade of Guards doesn't get off to a great start and after a few days of basic training it is already getting too much.

Budds Farm
15 October

Dear Charles,

I have had a really, nice encouraging letter about you from Andrew Napier; your Company Commander apparently thinks well of you, too. I'm sure you will justify the opinion of all, including myself and all your family, who have great faith in your determination and ability.

Jane sends her love, also Tony S.

RM

I am shamed into staying! On parade for the first time the Company Sergeant Major shouts over to me (to my absolute horror), 'You over there lad! Come over 'ere!' In my best attempt at marching I shamble over pathetically, sometimes even managing to swing both arms at the same time. The CSM addresses the entire parade ground of several hundred recruits: 'I've been at Pirbright now for twenty-five years and there is only one thing that makes my life worthwhile and that is getting a right little cripple like Mortimer 'ere and after twenty-four weeks turning 'im into an 'alf bleeding cripple!'

Budds Farm
24 October

My Dear Charlie,

Thank you so much for your letter. At least you seem to have retained your sense of humour, a quality that will help you to survive singularly disenchanting situations. I expect life is fairly tough and gritty but then it's meant to be. A soft soldier is rather less use to the community and to himself than a wet paper bag. We often think of you here and everyone has faith in your ability to see things through. Louise and Jenny send their love; when I told Mr Randall about your friend with ringworm and scurf he laughed so much that he let out an extremely loud fart and was slightly embarrassed. I have many enquiries about you from the Carnarvon Arms where a large coloured postcard from Nidnod decorates the bar. I really think Nidnod had shown immense pluck and resilience but there may be late reactions. I am consulting the Regional Crime Prevention Officer to see if I can tighten up security here when Nidnod is on her own. What a dirty rat Tony S. is to sneak about the Rover! I had some drinks with a man with one eye and I was driving Mrs Wright home when I backed into an iron post. Very annoying and don't tell Nidnod! I have been using her car and people I give a lift to keep on asking me what the sign 'Nidsky Nodsky' means on the dashboard. I say that your mother is a female freemason and it is a secret code sign. The other day I bought some sausages in Kingsclere, leaving the keys in the dashboard. Returning in heavy rain two minutes later I found the car had locked itself (the other doors I had locked at the station and had left locked). I could not get in and was desperate. I eventually did so but will not tell you how or you will tell Nidnod. I have been puzzled how to turn on the lights and open the bonnet but am gradually learning. Joanna Greenwell is here; her brother has a straggly beard, does not wash, stays in bed till lunchtime except on the days he works as a male charwoman. His parents are not entirely satisfied with his way of life but he says he is 'doing his thing' whatever that means; it sounds faintly rude. I saw Cringer in Newbury; he jumped into my arms and licked me rather too effusively. It is Mr P.'s fiftieth birthday on Monday and I am sending a fairly lewd card. I go to dinner there in the evening. No news from Jane who is less organised than ever and wastes her time making totally hideous handbags.

I must do some work. Keep your courage up and try and see the comic side. We are all on your side.

R

Clearly everyone else has a great deal more faith in me seeing things through than I do. My mother has just been badly beaten up in a robbery in Kenya and is showing considerably more resilience than I am. Generally speaking the women in my family are much tougher than the men.

Budds Farm
1 November

Dear Charles,

I hope all goes reasonably well with you and that you are keeping out of trouble. Is there any chance of you getting permission to come home next weekend and see your mother? I know it would give her great pleasure to see you. Also you could help me with the drive to Gatwick to meet her. I hope to get the Rover back soon; I suppose I had second place in the queue after Tony's father! I had dinner with Jane last week and met her friend Colin something, a lounging sort of fellow with unkempt hair like a yak's tail. Very trendy no doubt, but give me Paul Torday any day. However, that's not my business. I had drinks with the Greenwells in their flat. They lent me a large Jaguar plus chauffeur to take me to Gibson Square but after forty-five minutes I had only got to Hyde Park Corner owing to the traffic and bailed out. I have many enquiries for you here and say as far as I know you are still breathing and not doing detention. I trust I am right.

Yours ever,

D

I have soon learnt that the best way to survive is to trade what you are good at with someone who can cover areas in which you are lacking. I service the platoon sergeant's old Jaguar and in return my kit gets buffed up.

Budds Farm
13 November

Dear Charlie,

I hope you are still keeping your head above water. We all
think of you a lot and admire you for the way you are tackling
a life that is at present tough and demanding. Nidnod is very
nervous still and got into a really alarming flap when a police
car drew up at 8.30 p.m. last night and made enquiries about,
of all really dreary things, a missing bicycle at Tadley. This
very dim affair involved someone called Mortimer living at
Burghclere and I eventually convinced two exceptionally thick
members of the Hampshire Constabulary that I was not the
Mortimer concerned, nor were you. Nidnod got very aggres-
sive and thought they were burglars dressed as police, and
made me check with Basingstoke Police Station. All in all I
had a restless evening. Nidnod talks of buying a revolver, in
which case I think she is certain to pot a member of her own
family before long. However, don't tease her too much as she
is obviously suffering from quite acute shock reaction. The
builder is here today and found the floor in the loo by your
room quite rotten. In a matter of days someone would have
appeared feet first in the kitchen perched on the loo seat. Also
the supports in the cellar are rotten and the entire house may
collapse. Bankruptcy will stare me bleakly in the face after all
the repairs are done. Mrs Lewis, whose daughter you know,
cooled on Tuesday. I did not feel obliged to attend the funeral.
Dr Britz's small son died the following day, aged two. I have
just received another cheque in respect of the play and it is
just about keeping me going at present. I hope it will at any

rate run till Christmas. Uncle Ken has given his horse con-
cussion. I shan't go to lunch again there in a hurry. The house
is cold and there is SFA in the alcohol line.

RM

*I suspect that if I were to remain a squaddie, I would be
perfectly content. I make quite a few friends at Pirbright and
on the whole life is very entertaining: 'As for you Recruit
Mortimer you're marching like a donkey with an 'ard on!'*

Budds Farm
21 November

Dear Charlie,

Thank you so much for your cheerful and informative
letter. I hope your squad will not totally disintegrate in
the course of the next few weeks. I wish you luck in your PT
test; I got the lowest possible marks for PT at Sandhurst and
thank God never had to do any again afterwards. I think it is
a smelly and undignified pastime. We had a man from the
Hampshire Crime Prevention Squad round yesterday. His face
was concealed under gigantic mutton-chop whiskers. I think
he wants to install an electronic early-warning device here at
a cost of about £5,000. What a hope! Your mother and
Louise are hunting today and so of course there is a great flap
and general commotion on; I intend to keep well clear. Prince
Charles flew to a neighbouring airfield on Thursday and made

himself very agreeable. Not so his equerry, Soames, who was reported to me as incompetent, ill-mannered, uncouth and very badly turned out with filthy boots. The Secretary of the Cottesmore Hunt, whom I met with Aunt Pips, was killed out hunting last week, his horse rolling him very flat indeed. Jane is coming down tomorrow accompanied by Gale but not, I am happy to say, by her bobbed-haired boyfriend whose name continues to elude me. Ian has been here trying to mend a radiator; he has failed to do so possibly because Nidnod never stopped talking and did not permit him to get on with the job.

Yours ever,

D

After my physical training test, the sergeant reads out the names of everyone in our platoon and their respective grades but to my surprise I'm not amongst them. He gives a theatrical pause and then continues, 'As for you Recruit Mortimer you are merely interesting as a statistic.'

1971

19 March

Dear Charlie,

I hope all goes well. I sat next to Major Philippi's father-in-law at luncheon. He is known as 'Tadpole' Mead and has a son in the Coldstream. He said his son did very well at Pirbright but then got over-confident at Mons and dropped a term! The food was very good at the Popes and my liver took a lot of punishment. Nidnod drove my car so fast over a ramp that the wireless is now kaput. Louise has found a school where she can take her pony and do sailing + judo! She omits any mention of anything as crude as education.

No news of Jane. How does she live without working? I wish she would pass the secret on to me. I have hired a French girl to coach L in the holidays. I hope she is young and dishy and not one of those squat, hairy ones with Grenadier moustaches.

Work hard and don't drive too fast, please.

Yours ever,

D

I move on to an Outward Bound school (where incredibly I do rather well). One morning, leading a climb up an impossibly awkward cliff face, I am stopped in my tracks by an overhang. 'Sergeant, I'm stuck,' I shout to the rather gruff Grenadier Guard Instructor. 'Well get soddin' well unstuck then you soddin' little sheepshagger you!' is the unequivocal response. (The Grenadiers use the nickname 'sheepshagger' for Coldstreamers.)

Budds Farm
22 March

Dear Charlie,

I enclose a letter from CNCA; I had one, too. I went to Simon Sandbach's twenty-first birthday party and heard some news of you there via the Yarrows. I went to the Surtees wedding on Saturday. I hate weddings; they are so sad. The bridegroom had been found up a tree in Chelsea early that morning by a police patrol and narrowly escaped arrest. I gave your mother lunch at the Ritz first; it cost me a month's pay. Cringer made a big mess in the hall today and I stepped slap into it. I met an officer called Holdsworth-Hunt who had known you at Pirbright and oddly enough seemed to think well of you. I hope all goes well at Mons and that you are pleasing Major Fishpleasure of the Tank Regiment or whatever the name of your company commander is. The Closes move to Alton on 1 April. Jane is going to Greece for six months and so is Celia Toller. I am engaging a larky typist today. Uncle Chris was eighty yesterday; I feel it today.

Yours ever,

D

I am now a cadet at Mons Officer Training school in Aldershot. Our platoon sergeant introduces himself with, 'I call you Sir and you call me Sir. The only difference being you mean it, I don't.'

Budds Farm
23 March

Dear Charlie,

Thanks for your entertaining letter. I am glad life is endurable at Mons and that you have a few friends to laugh with. Nidnod has a sore throat and is a bit crotchety in consequence. Did you read that huge account of the trial and conviction (four years) of Pete's brother? Nasty for them all. I did a recording here yesterday for the BBC on the Grand National but it came out as if there was a pillow stuffed in my mouth so will have to be done again. I am backing Cnoc Dubh, because the owner is lucky (and owes me some money) and Sandy Sprite for a place (it is trained by May's brother-in-law).

Best of luck,

D

I manage to make one or two fairly disreputable friends while at Mons.

The Sunday Times
28 March

Dear Charlie,

It seems a long time since we last met and I do hope all goes well with you as I'm sure it does. Louise came home for the holidays with a temperature of 103 and has been in bed ever since, greatly to Nidnod's irritation as the plans for pony shows etc. have been cast into utter confusion. Your poor mother has a bad throat herself and is in poor spirits. Cringer has a chill and was sick in a peculiarly unattractive manner in my room yesterday. I went up to Doncaster and back on Saturday. I got a nice little seat in the luncheon car at an unoccupied table for two and was just getting my tongue round the Crosse & Blackwell's tinned asparagus soup when the waiter says, 'There's a young honeymoon couple who don't want to be separated and your table would do them nicely. Do you mind moving and I can give a single seat at a table with some very nice people?' Like hell you can, I thought, but shifted with ill grace to leave the table to a very dirty young man with a beard like black cotton wool and a dark lady with the promising beginnings of a heavy cavalry moustache. They may not want to be separated now, I thought, but I bet they soon will be. Off I trudged to the 'nice people' who turned out to be Lord Wigg and the lady from the Home Office who fulfils various functions in his life. If they were pleased to have my company, they concealed the fact remarkably well. The situation was not eased when I tried to pour out a glass of Vin du British Railways extrémement ordinaire when the train was doing 100 mph and sloshed it all over the table cloth. I stood the lady a glass of Benedictine that tasted as if it had been drummed up in the gasworks at Staines and this gesture was reciprocated by a lift to the races in the Mayor of Doncaster's Humber, Lord W. and his bird reclining on the Bedford cord upholstery at the back, I perched sedately in front with a very standoffish uniformed chauffeur. I think the chauffeur thought I was either Lord Wigg's valet – not a very efficient one judging from Lord W.'s turnout – or a rather elderly and decrepit private detective. However, my morale was slightly restored when a blonde lady with a nose like a chisel introduced herself to me in the Hyperion Bar as Edith Millercrap or some such name and stood me a large Irish whiskey which I naturally accepted. We had a lively conversation in which I was on the defensive at times, as for example when she asked, 'What on earth had happened to Renée and those awful twins and did they still live in Penge?' It would be interesting, and doubtless humiliating, too, to discover who she thought I really was.

I suppose you'll need a complete trousseau like a young bride when you become a 2/Lt. You can rely on me to cough up.

Best wishes and keep out of mischief,

D

I am now on the verge of becoming a 2nd Lieutenant.

8 May

I am still clearing up the mess of the remains of your military career. I enclose a letter from Lt/Col J. N. S. Arthur of the Greys. I do not know whether you have had the courtesy to write and remove your name from their list but I have informed Lt/Col Arthur myself that you felt the call to minister to lunatics rather that serve your country as a soldier. I assume of course you were telling me the truth when your spoke of your intention.

I have had a letter from Michael Kidson, one of your few friends that really seems to care about your future, deploring the utter folly of your decision. However, no doubt others among your friends, who shall be nameless, are delighted.

If you will give someone here your address, I will see that various communications are forwarded to you, including a registered letter from the military authorities.

Your mother is much better but she has you and your future on her mind for most of the time. The wound you caused by acting as you did without any warning to us or without the ordinary politeness of a son to his parents in asking their advice over a matter that was clearly very close to their hearts will take a long time to heal; perhaps it never will.

RM

My decision to leave the Guards when I am within a whisker of being commissioned is, not surprisingly, fairly unpopular within the family. My Uncle Ken (a full general and until recently Commander-in-Chief of Allied Forces, Northern

Europe) has this to say, 'You're what I call the bally limit!' He then booms, 'You're what I call a shy horse!' before offering me a glass of sherry. As for the platoon sergeant, he simply announces to the barrack room, 'It's Mr Mortimer. He's gorn an' thrown in his 'andbag.'

Budds Farm

Dear Lupin,

I went to Aunt Margery's cremation at Slough today. Present from the family were Aunt Joan, Cousin Tom and myself. Also there were Aunt Margery's companion Miss Craven and a very temperamental Irish cook called Bridie. While I was waiting I looked at the racecard and saw the first for the fry-up on Tuesday was Daisy Simmons; no relation of your friend from the garage I hope! We had lunch afterwards at a curious hotel in Gerrards Cross inhabited by old ladies of eighty-five or over and got slightly sloshed at the bar first. Cousin Tom, like all those above the nappy-wetting stage, thinks you have made a complete ass of yourself by walking out of Mons; and that your failure to inform your parents before you made your decision was utterly lamentable. But let that pass. I think Cousin Tom knew about it before I did; these things get around in an odd way. Informed of Aunt Margery's death, Aunt Shirley replied, 'She's been like that three times before but has always recovered.' The other day she suddenly ordered her old maid to wear a lace cap when dishing up lunch. Needless to say the maid did not own such a thing but honour was satisfied by her wearing a table napkin on her head when she handed round the stewed prunes and junket. Uncle Chris is desperately ill after a stomach operation, no joke for a man of eighty with a weak heart. However, he comes from a far tougher and more resolute generation than yours and mine so will probably survive. A lot of recorded deliveries (letters) seem to be arriving here for you. That can only mean you owe someone money or that your bank is getting worried. All I hope from you now is that you keep out of gaol, at least till after Jane's wedding, so if you are in difficulties, for God's sake don't go handing round any rubber cheques. Before I pay you your quarterly allowance on 1 July, I shall require to see your bank account to assure myself that you are not getting into murky financial waters. Uncle Reggie is getting very weak and weighs less than nine stone. I am off to see the Hambros new estate tomorrow. Mr Hambro has had to have two operations on what is left of the leg that was blown off in a tank in 1944 when serving with 4th C.G.

Your mother is very much better but worries about you the whole time. Please give her as little cause for concern as you can.

Yours affec.

RFM

P.S. A good deal of Aunt M.'s estate goes to Miss Craven who deserves it. Cousin J. gets less than anticipated. I draw up £100. Whoopee! Legacies have been left to hordes of god-children, most of whom are over fifty and are children of former cooks and housemaids at The Cedars before 1920. It will be hard to trace them.

The fallout from my rather sudden departure from the Army is subsiding and family thoughts are now concentrating on my older sister's imminent marriage.

Budds Farm

Dear Charles,

I suppose that writing a serious letter to you is about as effective as trying to kick a thirty-ton block of concrete in bedroom slippers, but I am a glutton for punishment as far as you are concerned.

I may be wrong – you tell me very little – but you seem to be drifting along in a thoroughly aimless fashion with no plans for the future at all. When I am asked what you are doing, I don't know whether to say 'part-time farm labourer' or 'second-hand car spiv'. The unfortunate truth is that in an era of growing unemployment, you have no qualifications and a poor record. I really think you would be well-advised to go to Australia for three or four years. It is a land of opportunity and you would not have your boring old parents breathing down your neck and hoping that, with maturity, you would show some sense of purpose and would become a bit cleaner and tidier!

I regret your relationship with your parents is rather unsatisfactory. Your mother really loved you too much when you were young, and the failures, shocks and troubles in recent years have hit her harder than you realise. That she is often tiresome and unreasonable with you is the direct result of her disappointment and the collapse of all her ambitions and hopes as far as you are concerned. Fundamentally, she is very fond of you still. If she cared less, it would be easier.

For myself, I am more philosophic, being by nature pessimistic and always anticipating bad rather than good. The Mons episode, though, coming as it did without warning from you, was a fearful blow in a great many ways; as I said at the time, it was the end of the road as far as our personal relationship was concerned. However, that did not appear to cause you to pause in your folly for even a fraction of a second. I was ready to back you to the hilt while you were in the Army; sometimes I find it hard to raise much interest now, but I am sufficiently fond of you to care about you becoming a mere waster.

I really think you ought to look ahead a bit and not live from hand to mouth. Don't rely on a fat slice of bread when I kick the bucket, as the way things are, there won't be much left and in any case your ration will be in a trust until you are thirty-five; or alternatively, until the trustees judge you to be a responsible person. I don't want my savings going on fourth-hand Aston Martins!

If you are staying in Devonshire, why not go and see Steve Russell, whose address Freddy Burnaby-Atkins gave you? The man I know in Cullompton is Tony Allen. He is about fifty-eight and was a great cricketer in his day and played the violin. His initial is A. W.

If you insist on trading in cars, be very careful both with your own cheques and with those you receive. You have been WARNED.

Yours ever,

D

It is now the summer of 1971 and I have rented the wing of a rundown mansion in Devon for the knockdown price of £4 per week. I travel down to the West Country employed as a salesman by a firm which markets an unusual formula of stainless steel paint. This post lasts all of a week before I am fired. I then take up farming (of sorts) and second-hand car dealing with local legend, Robin Grant-Sturgis.

30 October

Dear Charles,

It was thoughtful of you to give me those cigarette cards with jockeys on them and I am most grateful. I trust you are not yet disenchanted with your work as an agricultural labourer, a calling for which your costly education has no doubt suited you. However, as long as you are happy and not in serious trouble, who am I to complain?

I won £3 at bridge last night with old Lord Carnarvon, but your dear mother lost £4.60 at gin rummy and then expected me to pay which seemed a bit hard.

Yours ever,

RM

I am not sure if many other fathers would be quite so generous of spirit regarding their son's catalogue of failures under similar circumstances. Whilst I am trying to cash a cheque, the bank call my home branch and then ask me a few questions for identification purposes. Finally they ask to see

my hands. This seems to satisfy them. 'Just out of idle curiosity why did you need to see my hands?' I enquire. The response: 'Newbury Branch says you have the dirtiest finger-nails they have ever encountered.'

Budds Farm

My Dear Lupin,

Thank you so much for your great kindness in sending me such a well-chosen card for my sixty-second birthday; and will you please thank Mrs Grant-Sturgis for hers? I get the message all right. Your mother has given me a very nice travelling bag. I had a very uncomfortable night and felt as if my cock was full of red-hot gravel. This morning I 'passed' a large, smooth stone about the size of a negro's head and feel greatly relieved in consequence. How it got through I simply don't know but no wonder it provided a ration of truly delicious agony.

Yours ever,

D

P.S. Your Aunt Pam is really very unwell and we are all a bit worried. She woke up in the night unable to breathe and it could be heart trouble.

I regularly test the tolerance of my landlady Mrs Grant-Sturgis, whose housekeeper from time to time throws all my clothes over the first-floor balustrade because, 'They smell like a well hung pheasant.' By accident I unplug the deep-freeze in

order to use the socket for my new electric drill and fail to plug it back in, with predictable results.

Budds Farm

Dear Charlie,

I enclose a cheque for £12 which I hope will help. Please meet us at the Turf Club on Monday at twelve noon. Do NOT be late. If you can induce Mrs Grant-Sturgis to give you a manicure, so much the better. Your hands always look as if you had just been changing a bus wheel in inclement weather. I do hope you will be able to find work but times are unpropitious. There are a million unemployed, some with far better qualifications than you can ever hope to possess. Frankly I cannot see you spending your next forty years on the Stock Exchange. You can write to Roger Mortimer and Co if you like but it would be better for both of us if I did not become involved in any way. Unfortunately, for the last seven years you have been busily engaged in kicking the ball through your own goal, and now, to continue with football metaphors, you are facing a relegation problem. I fear there is little that I can do to help, and after the Mons fiasco with that weird story of devoting yourself to social service, it is better that I should stand clear. I know you are capable of hard work but so are about 790,000 of the unemployed. Possibly you will always be happier working for a wage than a salary but you know your own mind on that score. I assure you that I wish you well and if

you find yourself up to your front stud in manure, I will
endeavour to pull you out.

Yours ever,

RM

P.S. I have just read M. Kidson's magazine which includes my
article in it.

*Next year there is a party at the Turf Club is to celebrate my
parents' Silver Wedding. The following incident, I feel, sums
up their rather complicated and somewhat volatile relationship. My father has returned from Newbury races and has
his feet up in front of a blazing fire, surrounded by newspapers, a mug of steaming tea to hand, the six o'clock news
blaring from the radio. My mother has been foxhunting and
a horse has trodden on her face following a heavy fall. She
throws open the sitting-room door and just stands there,
a vision of mud and blood. My father casually looks over
the top of the newspaper and says, 'Do you know where the
biscuits are?'*

1972

Budds Farm

This is to assist in RENT and HOUSEKEEPING; NOT in wild orgies in the Camberley and Frimley area.

RFM

Budds Farm
22 March

Dear Charlie,

How are you doing? Have you got the tintack yet? I have engaged a really nice villa in Corfu from 27 August to 10

September. It is very expensive but a cook (Celia Toller type), a car, a speed boat and horses are thrown in. It has twelve beds and the Lemprière-Robins are coming too. If you could stand it, I would be delighted if you would join us – all free of course. Naturally you could be as independent as you liked.

I think a holiday in the sun would do you good and it would be nice to see a bit of you. Louise and Nidnod both hope you can make it but I shall quite understand if you feel it would not be your scene.

RM

The Crumblings
Much Muttering
Berks
10 May

Dear Lupin,

Your mother is still fairly seedy but is regaining her strength and is building up for a battle with your Aunt Pam who is calling here tomorrow. A man has spent five minutes tinkering with the washing machine and has just handed me a bill for £18.57. Thanks awfully! John Oaksey's father-in-law was killed near Great Shefford in a collision with a fire-engine. He was far from being a teetotaller. Now for a hearty laugh. A man rang me up from Fleet Street yesterday and told me that I had been awarded the 'Clive Graham Memorial Trophy' for services to the benefit of racing. (What services? you ask: answer have I none.) At all events I am now lumbered with going to London for a dinner and reception for 300 at the International Press Centre where the presentation will be made. I don't frankly enjoy that sort of thing and would prefer a couple of bottles of John Haig. Anyway, please don't mention it to anyone as it is supposed to be a secret at present! Old Lady Teviot who lived at Adbury is dead: I don't know her age but her husband would be 111 if he was still with us. The current Lord Teviot married the conductress of a No. 73 bus.

Yours ever,

T. Tightwad

Dad wins an award but is self-deprecating to the last.

1973

Budds Farm
27 January

Dear Lupin,

I expect business is as stagnant as the cesspit at the bottom of the garden so I enclose a small contribution which may assist you to pay your rent for a fortnight.

Yours ever,

D

Of course, it all goes on rent!

Budds Farm

I have got to go to the Newmarket Sales in filthy weather without my waterproof trousers and winter boots which I lent

you six months ago and you have not had the courtesy to
return.

If you wish to retain them permanently, the price to you as
a special concession is £12.

Since you aspire to be a property tycoon in outer suburbia,
you might practise businesslike methods in relation to bor-
rowing my clothes; unless of course appropriation is an
accepted part of the routine.

RFM

*I am currently working for a rather down-at-heel estate agent
in Ascot. Dad has worked himself up into a lather about some
missing kit he reckons he has lent me.*

Budds Farm
15 June

My Dear Charlie,

I hear you are moving to London and this may have
certain advantages. I naturally don't expect you to exist like
a constipated mouse there but please do not get heavily into
debt or run into trouble. I like Jeremy Soames but he is
probably far richer than you. He is also, I hear, fairly wild.
Fatty Soames is doubtless better equipped to cover up his
escapades than I am in your case. Andrew Brudenell-Bruce
has charm but he is at present a waster with no occupation
bar gambling. He comes into plenty of money soon and I

can think of someone who will very soon help him to get rid of it.

I don't expect invariable wisdom or discretion from young men; on the other hand I reckon it ought to be possible to steer clear of the more egregious forms of folly. If you do find yourself in manure up to your eyeballs, you had better apply here for help. You may not get it but you can never tell.

In other words try and have a good time without making a fool or a shit of yourself.

Your affectionate father,
RM

My father spots signs of more trouble brewing. There is some validity in his concerns.

I hope you are getting down to work and not wasting money playing the ass in London with George Rodney + similar types!

I think Prince Regent will win the Derby.
RM

In the event Morston wins the Derby by half a length.

Budds Farm
7 July

Dear Charlie,

I am told that you have been offered a new job by a reputable firm called Hamptons. No doubt you will be wise to accept it if the prospects for the future are reasonably good. I hope you will find somewhere suitable to live in London. I am not sure that I consider Maison Soames 'suitable'. Personally, I rather like Soames but I am disturbed that so many of his own age-group rate him as 'bad news'. I do not want you to be dragged into trouble or excesses. I hear that with a degree of folly that is hard to credit you permitted some child to drive your Fiat into a concrete wall. Doubtless Mr Addison in moments of exasperation used to quote to you: 'Sunt pueri pueri; pueri puerilia tractant.' I think Miss Blackwell is to ride in a race at Ascot in a fortnight's time. Mrs Hislop went berserk at the Loyd's ball; she kicked Lady Dartmouth up the arse and called her a 'dreary old bag' and then, after a brief argument, she punched poor old Dick Poole on the jaw!

Yours ever,
RM

To everyone's astonishment I am offered rather good job in St James's, London, with an upmarket estate agent.

Dear Charles,

Last night I had two long conversations on the telephone

with Mr Shearer. He agrees with me that this proposed jaunt to South America must not take place.

He spoke to me about his son with a candour that must have been painful to him. I gather that this boy of nineteen (or less?) has a lamentable record and was sent to an Approved School. He is still 'under care'. He is unfortunately, according to his father, typical of young persons involved in the drug scene in that he is incapable of speaking the truth and is devoid of moral values.

Surely, unless you prefer to remain wilfully blind, you must see that the poor boy is totally unsuited in every way to be your sole companion on an 'adventure' trip to South America? What do you know about South America? Can you speak the language? What are the political conditions existing there? What are the health dangers? Have you the money to transport yourselves and your car?

If you went off with this boy, I would be subjected to the constant worry of you both ending up in some sleazy South American gaol.

I am totally opposed to you going and Mr Shearer is totally opposed to the expedition, too. Of course, I cannot order you not to go and I cannot recollect any occasion when you have consented to take my advice. However, I regard this plan of yours as so undesirable and so potentially dangerous that it would be cowardly of me to wash me hands of the whole affair. If, therefore, you decide to go against my wishes on this occasion, you must be prepared to accept the consequences, which will not in the long run be to your advantage.

Mr Shearer told me a long and involved story about shares, I.O.Us and so forth. The impression I gained is that either you are some complete fool and allowed yourself to be used; or else, with your eyes open, you went perilously close to aiding and abetting a fraud. I found the whole story squalid and distasteful.

You are in many respects still very young for your age and I hope you will forgive me if I say you seem to have a regrettable propensity for picking up undesirable friends. You must try hard and steady down a bit. I know you were never any good at football but must you always try and kick the ball through your own goal? You are capable of working hard and effectively but since you were at Eton you have never been able to stick to anything. I am getting old and tired and I can't last forever. What sort of a head of the family will you be? Will you really be in a position to look after – or at least help and advise – your mother and sisters? You won't be much use if you are in Venezuela with a juvenile junky. Surely you are old enough to know that your mother is exceptionally highly strung and family worries can throw her off balance to an extent that is genuinely alarming. You must surely have known that you were going to upset her badly. The consequences are being borne by me, not by you.

I would be more sympathetic to your wish for 'adventure' if you had not walked out of the Army like a housemaid taking affront at some fancied slight. Had you remained, you might have had plenty of adventures and might have perhaps experienced them in the public good. Perhaps it is my fault that you find it hard to be frank with me and I cannot forget that you told me you left the Army as you wanted to look after under-privileged children. Perhaps Charles Shearer comes into that category in your opinion?

All this is to me very painful, distressing and worrying. I need hardly tell you that your mother is in a thoroughly disturbed state. My advice to you is to take up your job at Hamptons and stick to it. I am sure that any close association with Charles Shearer will end in utter disaster.

Yours ever,

D

I have just started my new job but within a week I resign, full of ambitious plans to go to South America with one of my more disreputable friends – the only boy, I think, ever to have gone straight from Eton College to borstal.

The Sunday Times

Dear Charles,

You certainly live up to the name of 'Lupin' but I don't yet know who is cast for the role of Miss Daisy Mutlar.

However, many thanks for your letter which at least was not abusive as I am given to understand your letter to Mr Shearer was. Possibly I am pessimistic by nature, but so far your career has hardly inspired a demeanour of sunny optimism. If there are signs of panic, as you infer, it is because certain past experiences left an indelible mark.

As regards your friends, you are quite right to be loyal to them. You must permit me, though, to possess my own judgement as to their 'desirability'. I do, though, like Chicken Hurt, who seems neatly cut out to be one of life's more agreeable failures. I know very little about Shearer junior. Perhaps one day you will have the leisure to explain to me why he went to an 'Approved School'; and the details of this curious financial transaction that seems to annoy his father so much.

I am sorry you are already disillusioned with your work as an estate agent. The job, though, was your own choice. It is easy to find a trite phrase that will devalue any form of employment. I have heard my own described as 'casting sham pearls before real swine'. I doubt if you will find any work rewarding unless you give thought as to what you can put into it; not just what you hope to take out. If the notion of sitting in an office repels you, why did you not go into the Army or the RAF or something like that? Presumably because any code of discipline, and that includes self-discipline, is abhorrent to you. I cannot see what Charles Blackwell's life has got to do with yours. I don't know if he is happy or the reverse.

If you wish to work (I repeat 'work') in South America, by all means do so. Approach the matter in an adult and professional manner, though, and not like a Lower Boy. Go to night school and learn the language. Study the trade conditions and labour situation in the country you propose to favour with your presence. Go to the Royal Geographical Society and find out all you can about Brazil, Argentina etc. Above all go to S. America by yourself and stand on your own feet; don't just go on a motoring beano with some feckless companion. You could well afford to spend a year or more preparing yourself for this venture.

However, all good horses run true to form and no doubt in a few months' time you will want to be a jockey or manufacture cut-price tambourines for the Salvation Army. However, it is your life and I know nothing I say or wish will ever have the slightest effect on any course of action you propose to take.

Yours,

RM

The Brazilian adventure is put on hold. Dad good-naturedly resigns himself to yet another of my rapid career changes. I remember once saying, 'I've got a great idea for a new business.' He replied, 'For God's sake don't tell me what it is, sonny boy, or I shall probably laugh so much that I'll make a mess in my trousers.'

26 September

Dear Charlie,

Herewith £100, I suggest – I don't expect suggestions to be accepted – that you buy an overcoat, some watertight shoes and some warm shirts. You might also pay some rent in advance and put yourself – temporarily – on a good wicket.

I had lunch with your godfather F. Fletcher today, a very gentle person, essentially kind. His marriage is disintegrating, he is in poor health and v. hard up. Your mother is v. tiresome at present and by 8.30 p.m. seems to have reached the point of no return.

If Aunt Joan asks you to supper, please go. She is not a very hilarious character but fundamentally benevolent and you could be the heir! She's much richer than I am.

D

(R. F. Mortimer)

1974

Budds Farm
28 February

Here is some treacle for your petrol. If there is anything left over, stand plump Miss Fisheyes a drink.

   RFM

I have just opened an estate agency called Tips Butler and Co in Kensington High Street. The backing money is provided by some highly suspect continental gentlemen. Due to the miners' strike and the three-day week, this turns out to be possibly the most unpropitious time in living memory to open such a venture.

Dear Charles,

Aunt Shirley, accompanied by her nurse-companion, had to stay three nights in a hotel in Dorset last week. Unfortunately Aunt Shirley had to get up several times in the night. Each time she went back to the wrong room and the climax came when she climbed into a bed already occupied by a honeymoon couple. The manager asked her to leave the next morning.

Yours ever,
RM

I am invited to my Great-Aunt Shirley's eightieth birthday celebrations at the Dorchester. I say, 'Hello, Aunt Shirley, it's a great party.' 'Yes it is, isn't it?' she replies. 'Whose is it?'

I fear I opened this boring communication to you by mistake. How do you like humping bricks? I expect it is more fatiguing that constructing halma boards but more profitable. Come and have a rest here soon.

RFM

After my estate agency goes bust I try my hand at labouring on a building site and making backgammon boards which, rather surprisingly, I sell to Asprey, purveyor of luxury goods.

Budds Farm
3 April

My Dear Lupin,

I enclose a small birthday present with my best wishes. I'm afraid it won't get you very far nowadays but you may be able to buy a gallon of petrol and a meal at a Chinese restaurant near the Tottenham Court Road.

It is regrettable that your twenty-second birthday finds you out of work and with scant prospect of employment. I did talk to Mr P. on your behalf. Unfortunately his organization will not consider anyone who does not possess a university degree. Furthermore, out of the thirty graduates selected, only one or two survive the preliminary training.

It is unfortunate that you possess no qualifications of any sort, not even a single humble A level. Furthermore, you have never stuck to anything long since leaving school, which hardly encourages a potential employer. I know you are capable of hard work and you have the useful ability of getting on with people, but up till now you have been, in racing parlance, a non-stayer. However, it is the way of life you have chosen and there is nothing that I can do about it. I am afraid that the construction of sets for Ludo, etc. will not get you very far. Do you know anyone in North Sea oil? That is where the big money is going to be before long. My own business, journalism, is in a sad plight and it is quite possible that Beaverbrook newspapers will fold up before the year is out. Have you considered the Church? There is much to be said for the quiet life of a country curate. Fortunately in the Church of England an ordained priest is not committed to any but the vaguest beliefs. Mrs Hislop wants a jobbing gardener at £1 an hour. I don't know if any other duties would be expected! How about butler to a rich Kensington widow? You can never tell how things will work out in a job like that. Possibly that well-known Hampshire plutocrat, 'Chicken' Hurt, needs a chauffeur-valet. Would you mind sorting out his smalls? Anyhow, I think (and hope) you have a capacity for survival but don't push your luck too far. The charm of youth does not last forever – or even for a very long time.

I had a very long letter from Jane but had to give up halfway through as I was unable to read her writing. Louise has taken up smoking and drinking. What next?

If you think I can do anything to help, let me know. The worst I can do is to tell you to piss off. Also let me know if you are in dire financial straits. You never know; you might have the rare good fortune to catch me in a semi-affable mood.

Your affec. father,
RM

It is my twenty-second birthday and the general prognosis on the career front is not optimistic. It's not helped by my recent arrest for attempting to eat my passport whilst drunk in the discotheque of the Hamburg to Harwich ferry.

Budds Farm
10 September

Dear Mop-Head,

You might like to take little Miss Fisheyes out for a snack so I enclose small cheque. I have just received an indecorous postcard from saucy Miss C. Toller so will look out something saucy by way of return. It is hot and sweaty here and I have just taken the dogs for a long walk.

Your affectionate father,

RM

Don't spend all the cheque on Woodbines!

Schloss Rudstein
Neuberg

Dear Lupin,

I trust you are surviving the rigours of a northern winter. Avoid frostbite if you can as the effects can be of a permanent nature. Peter Yarrow and his wife have opened a catering business near here; they are doing a dinner for us on my birthday. I finish with the S. Times tomorrow. Yesterday a keen young man, who knew P. Majendie in Paris, came and took about 119 photographs of me for publication on Sunday. As it was raining the whole time, my cap is too small for me and your mother was trying to cram the animals into the foreground, the result should be interesting. The photographer stayed till 2 p.m.; that did not worry me as I left at 12.30.

Your mother held him in riveting conversation. Your mother has been very nervy and difficult but is now better and trying hard to be calmer and to make sense. You stand high in her estimation – for the moment. Louise is very low and Jane is low, too. We went to Nona Wallis's wedding reception which was fairly unexciting. Your mother insisted on asking various people to dinner afterwards – an outburst of hospitality that cost me £25. I bought four new tyres today at a cost of about £70. I think they are made by Firestone Ltd, not a firm I care much for. I have bought quite a nice bedside table for your room. It may have been a po-cupboard once. As I shall be short of money from now on, I have put my name down with Camp Hopson to assist at funerals. I have to provide my own tailcoat and a dark overcoat. The important thing is not to carry the coffin always on the same shoulder as then the coat does not get worn and shiny on one side only. Your mother and I had a pleasant night at Brighton and we took Joyce out to lunch. She asked a lot about you. Your mother has met Mr Guinness out hunting and seems to get on quite well with him. I hope you will come down here soon and tell us of your experiences which I expect are curious.

Yours ever,
RM

I head for Scotland and find work on an oil rig. I am soon promoted from roustabout to the dizzy heights of roughneck. It doesn't take long before I acquire the nickname 'Jonah' from the rest of the crew as I always seemed to be at the heart of endless minor catastrophes . . . Dad hits sixty-five and retires from The Sunday Times.

1975

Budds Farm

My telephone bill has reached an all-time record as far as this house is concerned of £75. I find this impermissible in these increasingly difficult times; not least because I rarely use the telephone myself. I find myself reluctantly compelled to request all who use the telephone here to record for my information all calls not purely local (Newbury and District) and the cost incurred. Failure to comply will result in the number of telephones in this house being reduced from three to one.

T. Tightwad (proprietor and candidate for insolvency)

I have been back home, albeit briefly, and manage to cause the usual stress about the phone bill.

Budds Farm
7 January

Dear Charles,

I hope you are enjoying yourself and that neither you nor the young desperado you are with has run into serious trouble. We have been trying to spring-clean your room. I reckon Hercules would not have bellyached so much about mucking out the Augean Stables if he had had to have a go at your zimmer! There seemed to be sufficient equipment to start two quite big garages and enough wastepaper and empty cigarette packets to feed a bonfire of considerable size and power. Possibly because of my middle-class and military background, and a faint hankering towards a mild degree of cleanliness and order, I was slightly shocked. However, I have bought you a nice wicker dirty clothes basket (Ali Baba model), a five-drawer metal cabinet for your letters, receipts, writs, summonses, bills, lewd photographs, etc., etc., and a small fan-type electric heater so I hope you will be slightly more comfortable and better equipped. Your mother is tidying out your clothes and costumes tomorrow.

I had lunch with Sylvia Hambro yesterday and that Rolls-Royce will soon be available. She is very distressed because her eldest son wants to marry a tarty American divorcée aged about thirty-six and tough as a pair of Army boots. No news from Jane. Louise has been to two dances and is liverish. Cringer has worms and your poor mother continues to worry about everything and your future in particular. We had drinks with the Hislops on Sunday; the farouche appearance of the younger Hislop boy makes you look almost normal by comparison; is he rehearsing the part of St John the Baptist in a school play, do you think? Not much news in the papers; one member of a pop group ran over his own chauffeur and killed him, while a guitarist from another group has lost a leg doing something or other. Cousin John appeared on TV in a feature on Ian Fleming.

Don't do anything rash, and keep off the more sordid forms of self-indulgence.

D

Dad adopts a more mellowed stance towards my most disreputable of companions and my shortcomings generally.

Hypothermia House
Monday

Dear Lupin,

Thank you for your letter. I do not wish to pursue the correspondence in respect of the telephone bill. De minimis non curat lex [The law will not concern itself with such trifles]. Your mother has a nasty cold and is extremely crotchety in consequence. The Roper-Caldbecks are just back from a holiday in Devonshire. Owing to persistent rain they never left their hotel, which fortunately was warm and comfortable. We have had the big Budds Farm shoot, which proved a success. Three pheasants in varying stages of mobility were slaughtered between the rubbish heap and the top of the croquet lawn: after which the guns, or to be more accurate the gun, a boy of fifteen, retired for tea and crumpets. I have just been sent a book to review by the author, whom I greatly dislike. Hardly a single name is spelled correctly and the book is wildly inaccurate in every respect. There is an unfortunate reference to Mr Cottrill who hopes to be able to sue for libel. In the Sunday Telegraph there was a lot about Mrs Christian Miller of Newtown who at the age of fifty-four has gone round America on a collapsible bicycle. Farmer Luckes has had another stroke. An alternative route for the Highclere bypass has been proposed. If accepted, lorries will pass through our stable. Mr Parkinson is being driven barmy by his mother-in-law who is usually pissed and never stops talking the most fearful balls. A lady in Newbury has strangled her ever-loving husband with a dressing-gown cord. Jeffrey Bernard is in court at Newbury today over a combination of motor accident and unpaid debts. I think his wife has done a pineapple chunk. V. cold here today and thick ice on the water butt.

Yours ever

In a moment of wild desperation I agree to try my hand at attending agricultural college with a view ultimately to becoming a farmer. Instead, without warning and at the last minute, I become manager of a multinational rock band. This does not improve my mother's mood or anxiety level: 'What you need, my dear boy, is a raison d'être.'

Dampwalls
Burghclere
Newbury
27 June

Dear Lupin,

I think I forgot to tell you that the most immaculately dressed man I met in the Royal Enclosure at Ascot was the popular baker, James Staples. I had never seen him out of his red jersey before. It is quite peaceful here and I am watching a horde of rabbits and various birds of evil character destroy the garden. I am getting worried about the oil situation here next winter and am thinking of alternative forms of heating, including thick vests, longs pants and balaclava helmets. I had a reminder that the summer is passing when I received a request today to order regimental Christmas cards. I had dinner with the Parkinsons last night. I have rarely seen a garden with a richer crop of weeds. The Surtees garden is immaculate except where Major S. upset a can of weed-killer on the lawn. Mr Parkinson took some children (rashly, in my view) to the Air Display and had a truly horrific time. I think your mother is due home tomorrow. I have no news of any rows with Jane yet.

Your affec. father,

RM

P.S. I have been paid my fee by 'Pacemaker'.

Only my father could worry about the onset of winter in mid-June.

Budds Farm
23 October

My Dear Lupin,

I have received the enclosed letter from a Mr Sunderland, of whom I have never heard. Perhaps an impoverished literary hack like your father. If I have given you any family relics that would help, could you dig them out when you next come here?

I'm sorry to hear you are poorly. Are you getting enough to eat?

Yours ever,
RM

Mr Sunderland was putting together the history of our ancestor Sir John Hamilton Mortimer, RA. He lived in the eighteenth century, was a very successful artist and died from serious over-indulgence before he was forty.

1976

The Droolings
Much Muttering
Berks
11 July

My Dear Charles,

I hope your strength is holding out and that you are thus able to enjoy honest labour with well-earned relaxation. I have just been reading in The Times of fearful storms in the south-west of France. I have heard nothing of your sister and Hot Hand Henry. Can it be true that they are residing at a nudist colony on one of the remoter Greek Islands? It would surely be a weird choice for a honeymoon? Or perhaps not. Except for the first fortnight at their preparatory school a honeymoon is for most people the least happy experience of their life. Mr Parkinson woke up on the third morning of his first honeymoon and found that his ever-loving wife had done a pineapple chunk. I think Mr P. is scouting around for a fourth wife. If he does succeed in his quest, I hope I shall be best man again: it has become part of the tradition. I stayed with Cousin Tom last week. Among the guests were Sir D. Plummer, head of the Betting Levy Board, and Lady P. He is very ambitious and set on a life peerage: she is the epitome of Dorking and Reigate. Lady P. dipped her nut a bit too far into the martini bucket and became more or less unplayable. We got her up to bed fairly early and she kept on sending urgent messages down to her husband, intimating that he was to come up at once as she could not wait for him! (Why not? The mind boggles, whatever that means.) Next day Lady P. had a teeny bit of a hangover and looked like a pug recovering from distemper. We went to a very good midday party at the Herns yesterday where there was a lot to drink and your dear mother took advantage of that fact. Nor, in fact, did I stint myself. The Gaselees were there, Surtees, Walwyns and most of the Lambourn racing mob. A former jockey called Stan Clayton, who breeds budgerigars, was good enough to tell me all about his blood pressure, while a tall lady in an azure wig explained at some length why she loathed her husband so much. Perhaps I am a sympathetic listener: possibly I just lack the energy to move away. We had lunch at 3.30 chez Surtees where I dropped asleep with a glass in my hand and spilt the contents all over my new 'special offer' trousers. Of course, ill-natured persons suggested I peed during my brief period of repose which I am happy to say was an unfounded allegation. I am fairly busy signing bills is respect of Louise's party. Hire of the racecourse cost me £40, less that I had anticipated. I am not looking forward to the Blackwell wedding as I shall see too many relations. I slightly know the bride's parents. He is a rather stupid man but I think he has at least had the sense to avoid working. Mrs G. is one of Mr P.'s many ex-girlfriends, nice and bouncy according to Mr P. Jewish. I think an infusion of Jewish blood probably does most families good. For obvious reasons I hope so.

Your affec. father,

RM

My younger sister is now married and I am taking a well-earned break in the south of France with a little part-time chauffeuring thrown in for good measure.

Budds Farm
14 July

Dear Charles,

Thank you so much for the tastefully chosen postcard you so kindly sent me. It is grey and cold here and I have been stockpiling wood for the rapidly approaching winter. I am not at my best today as I think I have given myself a slight hernia bending down to cut my toenails with my gardening scissors. Your mother is rather crotchety but luckily is off to Jersey tomorrow for a boating holiday. I shall lead a relaxed life here, having meals when I like and looking at the TV programmes I like. Nor shall I be under any obligation to pretend that I am deaf. Pongo, thank God, is in a boarding kennel and all I need for happiness is some warm weather. Tomorrow I am off to stay with the Surtees and go to a play at Newbury. I have just received the bill for the reception: £429 is not exactly cheap considering it did not include £305 for drink. I have heard no news from Plump Louise and Hot Hand Henry: nor from Miss Bossy Pants up in Northumberland. I rather doubt if I shall go and stay at Brocks Clumps or whatever the Torday Château is called. The combination of your mother, your sister and two small children might be very tiring for someone of my age and delicate health. A Mrs Collingwood from Ecchinswell came to supper: her ever-loving husband has just done a pineapple chunk with a saucy nurse. There was a paragraph in the Newbury News that will not be greeted with hearty cheers by all concerned to the effect that a gigantic wedding is taking place on Saturday between a representative of the Gilbey family which churns out gin and the heir to the Blackwell fortune which is derived from baked beans! I remember some music-hall comedian being sued for libel for saying 'Any port in a storm – even Gilbeys!' I had a letter from Cousin John who is v. angry because Eton beat Harrow at cricket and considers this unexpected victory was achieved through blatant cheating by one of the umpires. The downstairs lavatory is leaking quite badly but otherwise the house is standing up reasonably well. Tiny Man's breath would drive a small car.

Your affec. father,
RM

A familiar theme: it's midsummer but as far as my dad's concerned it's time to get supplies in for the 'rapidly approaching winter'.

Dear Charles,

I hope you are settling down to the routine of therm-ometers, enemas, bedpans, hospital meals at queer times, other people's awful noises, tepid Horlicks and so forth. It is not much fun to start with but it is apt to grow on you insidiously. I expect the weekend will be unattractive as the hospital will be crammed with proletarian visitors, including many children of repellent appearance and anti-social behaviours. I hope there will not be a strike by the NUPE workers during your stay. They have the reputation of being extremely militant (in other words, bloody-minded) at Basingstoke and are under the leadership of a black female communist. Let me know if there is anything you need. I will come and see you tomorrow. Your mother is coming today and I know I should not be able to get a word in edgeways. I hope the doctors are adequate: I shall be surprised if you should see one that is not as black as ten feet up a factory chimney. Audrey has just fucked up my typewriter which has put me in a bad temper. She is a very agreeable woman but possesses a capacity for petty annoyance almost beyond belief. In some ways she is a sort of human Pongo whom I would willingly exterminate about ten times a day, though I would be filled with remorse afterwards if I did actually slay him. Not much local news: three people were roasted to death in a car accident at Theale. Mr Randall is back on duty, thank God.

Yours ever

R

Entirely due to excessive consumption of hard drugs and alcohol I am rushed to Basingstoke Hospital with liver failure. Dad's synopsis of hospital life proves fairly accurate. My mother (sometimes known as the Bureau of Misinformation) is desperately worried and following my liver biopsy calls a distant cousin who is a doctor for advice: 'I'm most frightfully worried about my son Charles, they've just done an autopsy on him.'

Budds Farm
18 November

My Dear Lupin,

I am so glad you are out of the woods and that your complete recovery is, with luck, just a matter of time and patience. You will, though, have to go slow for some time yet and take your convalescence seriously: no larking about. Cassandra rang up and may come and see you today. In the meantime, you will have leisure to plan in general terms for the future and devise some sort of scheme. Paul is in good form. Happily he is rising in the world with a speed comparable to that at which I am descending. I think he will end up with a château on the Tyne and as the local Master of Foxhounds. Jane will probably run the Red Cross and open bazaars in aid of the Conservative Party. Paul takes a fairly disenchanted view of Philps and thinks he is very tough and pretty hot, well capable of looking after himself. He (Paul) knows the man who bought the picture and rates him in the World Class as a creep. I gather the Tordays move into the wall-to-wall carpeted Castle quite soon. No doubt there will be a ball there (white ties: decorations will be worn). The more I see of Paul the more I like him. I wish I could repeat the remark in respect of HHH who in fact is probably no worse than a fearful bore who talks the most appalling drivel. However, he is apparently good at gutting rabbits (an example of Newton's Law of Compensation). Thursday is easily my favourite day as I draw my pension and for nearly twenty-four hours have an illusion of affluence. Cringer slept on my bed last night. His bad smells are so vile that they actually wake me up as effectively as a door being slammed. I see a Mrs Parker-Bowles married young Irwin yesterday. I wonder which Mrs P-B. that was? When I read of the goings-on in Parliament while the country sinks soggily into bankruptcy, I think that your Aunt Barbara would be entirely in place there. I am glad to say none of my family has ever demeaned themselves by becoming an MP. I believe your mother's uncle at one time represented Newmarket. He died of drink, thereby establishing a precedent followed by his wife and elder son. It is an expensive way of doing oneself in nowadays.

Try and keep reasonably cheerful (I'm sure Mr Boyce used to say 'Aequam memento rebus in arduis servare mentem' ['Remember when life's path is steep to keep your mind even']). You may never have another opportunity to lie on your bed after breakfast and read 'Playboy' or 'Whitehouse'. (Newton's Law of Compensation again?)

Your affec. father,

RM

I am finally due to leave hospital after eight weeks.

1977

Budds Farm
30 March

Dear Lupin,

I am delighted to have you living here and enjoying the modest facilities and comforts that your mother and I provide. All are free BAR THE TELEPHONE. If my name was Onassis I would probably (though not certainly) permit you to have free calls but frankly I cannot afford that particular gesture. Moreover I am by nature unsympathetic to all telephone users. Our last two telephone bills have amounted to some £275. The one received today adds up to £117.38p. I think my share of that is about 10p. I hope I am not being grossly unfair (a little unfairness is always to be expected in matters of this sort) if I charge you £50 as your share of the last two bills. A lot of your calls are due to Unimog and presumably can be charged to your firm, assuming there is sufficient money in the kitty.

Your affec. father,
RM

Convalescence at home has the odd hiccup, the phone bill being one of them. In a moment of insanity a friend buys 300 ex-Army Unimogs (four-wheel drive trucks) all stranded in a wood in Germany. He employs me as sidekick/salesman.

Budds Farm
1 August

Dear Miniwad,

I hope you are well and keeping clear of the more tiresome sort of trouble. I gave little Miss Bossy Pants lunch at the Ladbroke Club and she ordered smoked salmon mousse, the most expensive thing on the card! Also she ordered tomato juice but kept on taking jumbo swigs at my martini. Afterwards Paul joined us and we went to Heywood Hill's bookshop; then on to Major Surtees where he was in conference with some bibulous Dutchmen, one of whom lives next door to Paul's factory in Holland so they got on pretty well. For some reason or other I got on the wrong train at Waterloo but luckily I quite like Bournemouth. Hot Hand Henry complained to Jane that I don't like him. There is indeed substance in his complaint. In fact, I don't like any of his family but Louise chose them, not me. Your dear mother is endeavouring to live on a purely liquid diet with unfortunate results. One evening she popped my dinner into her car and drove off with it, saying she was going to give it to the poor! I was a little surprised, therefore, to find she had dropped it at the Bomers. The next night with unerring aim she threw a fairly revolting plate of charred mincemeat over my chair. Stirring times indeed! We went to a big lunch at the Roper-Caldbecks yesterday. Your mother is mad about a short man called Lloyd-Webber whose wife has diabetes. Mrs Boxall has gone to live in Hannington. She is due to marry again soon but the child is likely to be born first. I believe the husband-to-be writes TV scripts (a polite expression, usually, for being unemployed and short of treacle). I went to Goodwood which is v. democratic these days. In the Richmond Stand I saw a stout lady remove her shoes in order to massage the huge expanse of her escort's stomach. His response was minimal judging from the lady's language which was very frank indeed.

Your affec. father,

RM

Expect you back in the autumn.

My mother is christened 'Meals on Wheels in Reverse' after she removes Dad's dinner and delivers it in her car to our rather surprised neighbours.

Budds Farm

Dear Charles,

In the lavatories of my preparatory school someone had written up on the wall the time-honoured couplet:

'How eager for fame a man must be
To write up his name in a W.C.'

How eager for fame (or something) a man of twenty-five must be to give, unasked presumably, an imitation of a defunct pop-singer during an auction in London. However, few of our relations, fortunately perhaps, see the Daily Mirror. The Daily Telegraph kindly concealed your name.

I have no particular feelings about your performance beyond finding it, as I find most amateur entertainments, mildly embarrassing. I trust the incident will not affect your election to the Turf Club: some people may not have cared for it all that much. However, if you are blackballed, then it will give me the excuse to resign myself and join some dinner club more in keeping with my diminished income.

I have not entirely avoided publicity myself and saw myself described in some publication as an 'engaging raconteur', which is doubletalk for an egocentric and longwinded bore.

I trust that you are keeping moderately well and finding the occasional odd job to keep you partially occupied.

Your affectionate father,

RM

In honour of the sudden and premature demise of Elvis Presley some antique-dealer friends bet me £300 to jump up on the display table at a big Sotheby's sale and give my impersonation of 'The King' singing 'Blue Suede Shoes'. It is an essential component of the bet that a lot of leg-shaking is evident. My father is frankly unimpressed. However, I do make the front page of the Daily Mirror: 'Cheeky Charlie goes for a song.'

Dear Little Mr Reliable,

Thanks a million for doing the wood baskets as promised. My word, your employer is going to be a very lucky man!

D

It takes real skill and irony to craft such an effective dressing down in so few words.

1978

Budds Farm
26 August

Dear Lupin,

I am delighted, even if slightly surprised, to hear that you are adding cricket to your growing list of accomplishments. I shall watch your performance at Burghclere with much interest. I hope you peppered the grouse successfully and did not perforate your fellow-guests to any marked extent. Your mother enjoyed her trip to Jersey and returned bringing a crab the size of a whippet tank. It needed a sledge-hammer to crack the shell. At Whitchurch yesterday three men forced their way into a house at lunch-time, tied up the occupants and removed all the kit of any value. Martin McLaren's brother dropped down dead on holiday in Scotland. Pongo has been unwell and the vet has put him on a most expensive diet. We had drinks with Mrs Hislop yesterday and for once your mother was utterly out-talked. The Dowager Lady de

Mauley bred Totowah who won the big race at York at 20/1. I spent the morning cutting down weeds and brambles: unfortunately the belladonna (I think) proved allergic to my skin (or vice versa) and my arms have come up in purple golf balls, which is disconcerting. We are having dinner tonight with the Gaselees: I hope we don't get mixed up with the Lambourn Festival, which is in full swing. Little Miss Cod's Eyes has got Lizzie Jamieson staying with her. The Basingstoke dustmen have been on strike for three weeks and you can now smell that revolting town two miles away. I fear we may be in the throes of a General Election soon. I think it would be better to have one year of total boredom with a General Election, American Presidential Election, the Election of the Pope, the World Cup and the Olympic Games. Any spare time on TV to be filled by show-jumping and by groups of earnest parents discussing either sex-education for children or the problems of bringing up a family of spastics. I have just discovered my passport is invalid; so is your mother's but it was not noticed when she arrived at St Malo last week! I hope there are not a lot of Arabs in SW6 or sooner or later you will come under fire. I remember the panic in SW1 in 1921 when Field Marshal Sir Henry Wilson, an awful old shit as a matter of fact, was shot in Eaton Square by a one-legged Irishman. A lot of people who had served under Wilson in the war wanted to get up a subscription for the man who had potted him. Wilson was in uniform but unfortunately his scabbard was rusty and he could not extract his sword to have a slash at the assassin.

Your affec. father,
RM

P.T.O.

The most interesting murderer I ever met was Ronald True who did fearful things to a woman in the Fulham Road area. He could be quite amusing but suddenly it would become apparent that he was totally bonkers. You ought to read about his case. Mrs Willett (the first one) had her fridge repaired by that vampire man who melted down Mrs Durand-Deacon into sludge. I met at Aldershot a gunner officer's wife who had murdered her loving spouse with strychnine put into some roast partridge, but it could never be proved. The murder Oscar Wilde wrote about in 'The Ballad of Reading Gaol' was a Lifeguardsman who cut the throat of a lady working in the Eton Post Office.

I am (for some extraordinary reason) asked to play in a cricket team by a well-known local impresario against the cast of the musical Evita. To everyone's shame I am forced to bowl underarm to complete an over and am caught out first ball by 'General Perón'.

Chez Nidnod
26 September

Dear Lupin,

We are off to France this evening so a certain degree of flip-flap on the part of your dear mother is only to be anticipated. The cottage seems to be in demand. Yesterday a plump, jolly young man came down and I found he is the son of an old friend of mine, Pat Rathcreedan, who lives at Henley. The young gent, whose name is Thornton, owns a horse and a wife and wants to settle down here. Old Lady Norrie, whom I knew fifty years ago, wants to have a look round, and a couple from Sussex called Andrews have offered £27,000 (subject to survey, of course). They are in the thirties and seem respectable middle-class. We had dinner chez Surtees on Sunday. When they went to their villa in Elba, they found it had been broken into, vandalised and stripped by American and German hippies. They spent a week on hands and knees scrubbing up unspeakable filth. The hippies prowled around outside accompanied by large and extremely ferocious dogs. Anne Surtees did not dare go out by herself.

It has been v. hot and on Sunday we sat outside drinking champagne with the Bomers. The Grissells stayed here, neither in good form. I have evicted a platoon of exceptionally hairy and hostile spiders from our bathroom. The effort of producing a baby seems to have exhausted HHH more than Louise! Your godfather F. Fletcher is doing well as a pottery-mender: I have seen some of his work. It has been a good blackberry season and I have picked a lot, accompanied by an amiable bullock who now answers to the name of Nigel.

Your affec. father,
RM

Pure bliss for my dad is a bottle of chilled champagne, on the terrace, with our neighbours.

Thank you so much for your contribution to the dinner last night. I enjoyed myself very much though I did not much fancy Nidnod's driving on the way home. I prefer it when she is not being a female Fangio.

I'm sorry about your ulcer: it is hell not feeling well at your age. At mine, I'd die of shock if I felt anything but half-dead.

RM

To describe my mother's driving as hair-raising on occasions would be an understatement.

Château Gloom
Burghclere
Sunday

Dear Lupin,

I trust your stomach is more or less under control and that you are deriving a modicum of benefit from those expensive pills. It is cold and damp here and both boilers have been behaving in a typically erratic manner. I did some baby-watching for the Bomers last night (the baby is eleven years old) and your mother departed for a beano at Inkpen. I think gin was in fairly abundant supply there and it had the customary effect of making your mother behave like Queen Boadicea on her return home. There are now three deaf people in the house – Moppet, Pongo and myself. It is sometimes fortunate that I am unable to catch everything said to me. Your mother is still convinced that a poltergeist whipped away a sausage she was cooking and I expect she will call in the Rev. Jardine for consultation. A lot of policeman descended on Mr Luckes's house yesterday but I have been unable to find out why. I thought I had the cottage sold yesterday but your mother interfered at the last moment and now I am somewhat doubtful. Your Aunt Barbara is going to Jerusalem for Christmas; that ought to precipitate a new war in the Middle East. Aunt Joan goes into hospital tomorrow. I imagine David Willett is having an exciting time in Persia: my godson Richard Rome, married to a Persian, is there too. Newbury is full of people from the council estates in Thatcham doing their Christmas shopping. It would hardly be true to say that they add to the charm of the town. The tall woman with bandaged legs in the chemists in the Mall is going into semi-retirement: a sad loss, as she is easily the most reliable medical advisor in this area, particularly sound on skin blemishes and diarrhoea. A man was killed on the road at Beacon Hill on Friday: road conditions were disagreeable at the time. Mrs Cameron stayed on Thursday night: she and your mother talked incessantly; neither listened to a word the other said which was sensible as neither was saying anything really worth listening to. I had a long letter from your Great-Aunt Phyllis but could not read a word of it bar my own name and her signature.

Your affec. father,

RM

P.S. A long article on Dr Philips in the 'Newbury News'. A man from Gowrings has bought Brig. Lewis's house. The bearded man in the Newbury bookshop claims to have flogged 150 copies of my book which would be good news if I happened to believe it. Which I don't. The rather lanky young woman who worked in Jacksons in the afternoon has disappeared. I have kept a first copy of The Times for you. It might one day be valuable. 'Colonel Mad' has vanished from Lambourn: some say to gaol, others to a loony bin. Nick Gaselee won a nice race last week. There was a large photograph of him in the Sporting Life. Mr and Mrs Cottrill are off to India for two months. Mrs Randall is giving her relatives potatoes for Christmas. I have given up smoking.

I am in Fulham scratching a living from some part-time work driving articulated lorries having managed to obtain an HGV1 licence – my only serious qualification to date. My mother's drinking habits and subsequent behaviour come in for a certain amount of scrutiny.

Chez Nidnod
10 October

Dear Lupin,

I have just received a telephone bill for over £100. As you now seem to be a moderately successful property developer, would you care to contribute a small sum?

Your affec. father,

T. Tightwad

(This month's theme song: 'Buddy, Can You Spare A Dime?')

I try my hand at property renovation. My phone use continues to irk my dad.

Budds Farm
5 November

Dear Miniwad,

I hope you had a safe journey and were not completely exhausted on arrival. Rest as much as you can and don't tire yourself by arguing the toss with little Miss Cod-Cutlet. A summons arrived for you this morning: you certainly keep F. J. Thriblow, our popular postman, busy. Do see if the highly respected P. Torday, Hexham's favourite tycoon and sportsman, can advise you about getting employment once you feel strong enough to contemplate the prospect of work. As you will soon enter your twenty-seventh year, it is surely time you left your starting stall and participated in the rat-race. Either that or you must have a fat win in the pools. I seem to have sold (or rather my agent seems to have sold) a very drab book to a publisher called Macdonald of whose previous existence I was unaware. I hope his name proves to be Mosenthal as I much prefer to do business with a Jew than with some tight-lipped, bare-arsed Scot.

Your affec. father,
RM

I visit Hexham where my dear older sister makes extensive use of my rather basic DIY skills. There is a vain hope that my successful brother-in-law will somehow point me in the right direction for a rewarding and fulfilled life.

Chez Nidnod

Dear Lupin,

I fear you are not going to like this communication much as I am going to ask you to do something for me. Such requests are almost invariably boring. The situation is that I am worried about Aunt Joan. Her arthritis is getting worse and she is becoming increasingly immobile. It looks as if she will have to have a hip operation. All this makes life difficult for a woman of over seventy living on her own. Shopping has become a problem for her. Could you please go to Harrods or some such place and buy £25 worth of useful groceries for her? You could either have them delivered (Mrs Cockburn, 25 Vincent Court, Seymour Place) or you could drop them yourself. I leave the choice to you. I enclose a goose's neck for £30. Buy a bottle of whisky for yourself.

Your affec. father,

RM

Did you see that Croome won at Towcester on Saturday?

Aunt Joan is one of life's eternal Girl Guides and not exactly a barrel of laughs.

1979

21 January

Dear Lupin,

I was glad to hear you arrived safely and have met your cousin (or very nearly your cousin). Please give her my love. The weather here continues to be uncouth and the snow has been lying around deep and crisp and even. Actually it thawed in places yesterday and your mother was able to hunt. To her chagrin, she was brought down by a small child on a grey pony, but happily nothing was dented bar her dignity. Her arm is painful still and furthermore she has an abscess in her nose and a couple of mouth ulcers, all of which very understandably make her temper a trifle on the short side. I hope she will consult Dr Keeble tomorrow if he is not on strike, which almost every public employee seems likely to be. Poor Jane is snowed up and for several days Brocks Bushes has been without heating or light: not very comfortable. She was due to fly to Paris tomorrow with Paul but strikes and the weather have put a stop to that. I have been reading the proofs of a book of mine due out in April. The lady who compiled the index must have been pissed when she did her work: no sober individual could have done such a lamentable job. I have just sent in a note of protest that will ruffle a few feathers (I hope). The Surtees are giving dinner for twenty in their barn on Saturday. I trust the heating arrangements will be adequate or I foresee a few deaths from hypothermia. Your mother is not on speaking terms with Aunt Pam, diplomatic relations having been severed following a rather blunt letter about your mother's predominantly liquid diet. Mr Parkinson lunches here today. He is dead windy that his mother-in-law, a neurotic alcoholic, is planning to become a permanent boarder with him. Aunt Joan has just written to say how useful those groceries have been that you delivered to her. She does not go out yet in bad weather as she is nervous of falling. Old Luckes is back home, very much thinner and a good deal more gaga. Mr Mayhew-Saunders has been given a helicopter by his firm. I remember before he married his future father-in-law rated him the stupidest officer in the Navy. Mr Randall has been poorly: Mrs R. says he lives on strong tea and cigarette smoke. As he is seventy-four the combination seems to suit him. My last book has had a very good review in the Financial Times which may help to sell about three copies. I have had a long letter about finance from Keith Barlow, very little of which I understand. He is, if anything, more pessimistic than I am. There is no shortage in the shops here though Jacksons say they may run out of loo paper and firelighters. Yesterday I cooked my own lunch and was just settling down to it when

I saw a monster slug clambering up on a sausage. How on earth did it get there? Your mother is quite worked up about the strikes and is keen to go out with a rifle and pot a flying picket. She really is quite capable of doing it! I was nearly slain on the Sydmonton–Kingsclere road. A van came so close that it removed my offside mirror. No sign of anyone moving into the cottage yet.

Your affec. father,

RM

P.S. I do hope you are feeling better.

I am now residing in Kenya on the island of Lamu and partially employed as boat boy/mechanic by the local hotel. Life is joy itself and I am looking after a friend's pet monkey.

Budds Farm

Dear Lupin

Thank you for your excellent and informative letter. I am glad you are having a reasonably good time and hope your stomach aches will gradually disappear. It has not been a desperately amusing month here what with one thing or another. If you commit suicide you cannot get disposed of, as gravediggers and cremation workers are on strike. Well-meaning middle-class ladies are queuing up for voluntary work in hospitals: they picture themselves dishing up lunch to dear little children and it comes as a painful surprise when they are asked to help with a ward of hideous adult lunatics who cannot feed themselves and have to have their clothes changed every few hours like a baby. We went to a large drinks party at the Gaselees: there were a lot of people in a confined space and I could not hear a word anyone said which may not have been an intolerable deprivation. Afterwards we had supper with the Surtees at the Swan, Great Shefford, kept by a somewhat enigmatic character called 'Jamie' who greeted me with an effusive bonhomie which I could well have dispensed with.

We had two courses and a bottle of plonk: bill £30, which is fairly steep for a country pub.

On Friday the Hislops went to Sandown. On going to their car at 5 p.m. they discovered that Mr H. had put the keys into the pocket of a coat which he had unfortunately left in the self-locking boot. They had to hire a car in which to get home and the next day Mrs H. had to take a Newbury taxi to Sandown with the spare keys. Mr H. was <u>NOT</u> very popular. I saw Fitz Fletcher at the Parkinsons. He had been completely marooned for three days in Somerset with no water. The Surtees have got a new car, a red Volvo of immense length that would make a serviceable hearse. Poor Major S. is having trouble with his partners, one of whom who is only absolutely sober on fairly rare occasions and suing the firm over some grievance. The cottage has now been sold and paid for; the builders are busy gutting it completely. Farmer Luckes is in poor form and just sits staring into space. The Hurt's house in Derbyshire is the feature article in the current number of Country Life. Unfortunately there is no picture of the Chicken. The dishwasher has broken down and the young man your mother hired to mend it made things a great deal worse. Mr Randall went up to London and saw the Esther Rantzen show which he greatly enjoyed. Not much news of Louise or HHH; or of Jane for that matter. I thought I had received a rather nice invitation to dinner today but on closer examination I saw it was meant for Major Hamer who has been dead for seven years. However, my bookmaker has invited me to oysters and champagne in London. He is a good old male chauvinist (a bit King Lear, in fact) and never invites women to his better parties. Your mother bought some fish in Reading yesterday: it tasted a bit odd and we both had a very bad night. The de Mauleys came to lunch last week: Lady de M. is putting on weight and Gerald is clearly not a member of the local Temperance Association. Do you remember the Philips at Winchfield. He has just left his ever-loving wife after thirty-two years and proposes to marry some woman he met in the local lunatic asylum where he spends a fair amount of his time. He once jumped in front of a taxi.

Your affec. father,

RM

Yesterday I met an old buffer in Newbury who had been at the Gaselee's party. He tried out a new hearing aid there, switched it on to a maximum volume and has been stone deaf ever since.

The Danish family for whom I work in Kenya love my dad's letters so much that when they arrive I am requested to read them out to a small audience on the hotel veranda.

Budds Farm
23 February

Dear Lupin,

I have not heard from you for many a long day but assume you are still alive and in the Continent of Africa. Not much news from here: the weather has improved and I trust the worst is over. I had two dead elms taken down last week: the cost of felling, cutting up and stacking was £370 (less £40 for immediate payment). On the other hand we got about £250 worth of wood which will keep the home fires burning for a bit. I am getting very gaga or, more accurately, more gaga. On Thursday I drove from Murray and Whittakers with my briefcase (containing my pension book) on the roof of my car! Being deaf I did not hear it drop off. Luckily it was picked up by an honest schoolgirl who rang me up later in the afternoon. I rewarded her with a large box of chocolates. Her family all stood and stared at me as if I was a freak escaped from a circus. Yesterday I went to Eton and had my hair cut. Afterwards I went to the grocer's and bought a sausage roll for lunch. On returning to my car I could find no keys. I went back to the hairdresser's: no luck. The grocer's had shut for lunch. However I rang them up and they found the keys on top of some cheese. In the evening Nidnod dragged me off (v. unwillingly) to some ghastly fundraising beano at Uffington. It was a nightmare. On leaving your mother was blotto and drove the car forwards instead of back with the result that the front wheels got stuck in glutinous mud. I thought we would be there all night. I did NOT enjoy the drive home. Jane is not coming to the christening tomorrow but Paul is due here tonight. Last week I met old 'Spider' Jacobsen who is about 102 and lived at Budds Farm before the war. He told me he bought the place for £2,200 and built the cottage for £350! Nidnod has bought some expensive new kitchen equipment, the sole result of which has been to burn her hand quite badly. Aunt Pips had a burst pipe which flooded two rooms. It is a squash in the garage with your car there. I scraped my own car, backing out in a hurry, against the garage door; cost of repair, £300. Thanks awfully! I hope Nidnod is sober for the christening or I foresee a punch-up at the font with Lady K. I hear Peter Carew is behaving like a fool and is trying to get himself court-martialled. It seems a pointless method of getting out of the Army.

Your affec. father,

RM

P.S. I am busy writing an article on the Daily Mail to be published in Arabic in the Lebanon!

My father's account of the middle-class existence of a long-suffering, elderly gentleman in Berkshire, together with his self-deprecating humour, continues to prove to be a big hit in Africa.

Dear Lupin,

When you next see the Field Marshal will you please give him Mr Parkinson's kind regards. Apparently they were chums at Sandhurst just before the war. I have had a delightful morning firstly cleaning out Cringer's run and then scraping the dirt off my typewriter which carries a little plaque with the inscription 'Underwood Speeds the World's Business'. Hardly true in my case. I have bought a new carpet for the sitting room and have received a crushing demand for income tax. We lunched on Sunday with Bobby Kennard who was completely boracic lint until ten years ago when he netted a rich widow as his third wife. He lives in some comfort but is constantly reminded of his position just to keep him in his place. On Saturday we went out to dinner but our hostess had quite forgotten she had invited us. There was a tiresome man there who claimed to have been secretary to some Prime Minister. He drank copiously and was a monumental bore. The Surtees have just gone to some Spanish island with a tall man whose wife recently (and I believe with good reason) did a pineapple chunk. Yesterday I was accosted in Newbury by a lady in a red wig who claimed to have known me many years ago. I leapt into my car and drove off at high speed before she could inflict any embarrassment on me. Your mother is off to Martin McLaren's funeral on Thursday. On Sunday we go to a party at the Cardens'. Lady C. has some odd Welsh name like Eggfroth. Did you read about the bizarre case of the lady who took an overdose of hormone pills? Within twenty-four hours she was covered in hair like a gorilla and then she expired.

Your affec. father

Back in Fulham I am renting a room from a friend whose father is promoted to Field Marshal. While mildly inebriated we compose the following congratulatory telegram:

This morning seated on the pail
I chanced to glance the Daily Mail
A new Field Marshal for the nation
Quite relieved my constipation
Congratulations from your sons
Joe and James two idle bums
And Mort the Sport would like to say
Let's crack open a bottle of Pol Roger

Understandably, the Field Marshal does not find it all that hilarious.

The Shambles
Burghclere
Newbury

Dear Lupin,

It is very quiet here with your mother in Jersey. I was left with about a thousand instructions about dealing with the cat, the birds, etc. and I think I have forgotten most of them. I had a peaceful weekend chez Surtees, good food and a high standard of comfort all round. I think the Bomers are in Kent and Farmer Luckes is in Jersey. (Thinks: has he done a bunk with Nidnod? Nothing would surprise me nowadays.) Guy McLaren has died suddenly in Scotland. I hear your distant cousin Phil Blackwell cooled recently. He passed the last fifty years of a blameless life writing a history of the Blackwell family. I believe he had almost completed three chapters. I had lunch on the train to Basingstoke last Friday. Unfortunately it went so fast that I had not finished lapping up the 'potage du jour' when we pulled in at Basingstoke. The Surtees are off on what Germans call a 'Kulturfahrt' to Florence: there is nothing I would loathe more. The Parkinsons are off on a 'tour gastronomique' of Normandy. We have quite a lot of apples on two trees and Randy Randall has hinted at plums but I have not yet seen any. Audrey managed to smash up a fair amount of kit while she was here: a good horse always runs true to form. I hope you enjoyed Scotland (a loathsome country, in my opinion) and did not pepper any of your fellow guests. It is very easy to do so with grouse coming towards you. I enjoy eating dead birds but don't really want the bother of killing them. Cringer has killed three rabbits, two of them dazed with terminal illness and the third about four days old. However, he is very truculent and now seems to regard himself as a sporting dog. I came upon the following phrase in Bagehot's 'The British Constitution': 'There is nothing more unpleasant than a virtuous person with a mean mind.' Very true, in my opinion, and I could quote several examples. Fitz Fletcher went to a buffers' luncheon given by your mother's – and the first Mrs Parkinson's – old boyfriend (to say nothing of being the second Mrs Parkinson's third husband) – I am getting muddled, but he is an alcoholic ex-airman called Bill Boddington. The main course was curried turkey which gave one and all acute food poisoning and in fact several guests were put into 'intensive care' in the local hospital. The local stomach pumps were working overtime. The Basingstoke dustmen are on strike and have been so for three weeks so I feel no desire or obligation to tip them at Christmas. I have come to the conclusion that I hate publishers: they combine inefficiency in their public duties with intolerable complacency over their private lives. I dislike them, in fact, almost as much as naval officers. I once caught crabs off a naval officer's wife called Myrtle who had red hair and a hint of B.O. – and when I say 'hint' I am giving her the best of the argument. I hear the lovesick bloodhound is living in Lambeth with Paddy Hadfield. I take it that Paddy H. is female: not that it matters much these days, so many people seems to ride under both rules. We had a barbecue the other evening: at my age consuming charred pork chops and Co-op Chianti in a searing north-east wind provides only a modicum of pleasure. Tomorrow I am sending off for my winter wardrobe by means of a number of special offer advertisements.

Your affec. father,

RM

I am now trying my hand at painting and decorating. While driving to a job in Lowndes Square, my current business partner turns to me and says, 'I quoted £110 for the chasing . . . Tell me, Chas, what exactly is chasing?' Dad is full of news, much of it about his prisoner-of-war friends. He is clearly not a great fan of Scotland where I am invited (rashly, in my opinion) grouse shooting.

Chez Nidnod
20 September

Dear Lupin,

I enclose some tickets for the usual old draw. Best of British Luck! It is sweaty hot here and yesterday we sunbathed and had a picnic. We had caught seven moles during the last few days but the invasion has not been halted. I expected they would start coming up inside the house soon. Your mother hauled me off to the Newbury Agricultural Show where I was rewarded with a glass of tepid Cyprus sherry in the presidential tent. I purchased a hamburger sandwich; it was like eating a warm slug. I bought a kitchen knife from a Pakistani who looked as if he was just starting smallpox. The Cottrills gave us dinner at the Swan at Great Shefford kept by a former Daily Express journalist. It was very good – particularly the grouse. I'm glad I was not faced with the bill. Peter Walwyn told me he had killed 400 moles on one of his gallops, all in traps.

Your affec. father,
RM

A keen gardener, my dad has something of an obsession with attempting to exterminate moles. On one occasion he bought, by mail order, some 'special offer' mole bombs, from which he mistakenly stood 'downwind' and ended up in the local A&E.

Budds Farm
30 October

Dear Melville Miniwad,

Would you like to come to the annual beano of the racing press that takes place on 13 December at the Dorchester (12.45)? If you are unable to get away I shall of course quite understand. However, I think I can guarantee a fair tuck-in and a good laugh if you come.

Your affec. father,
RM

The Crumbling Pile
Berks
Dear Charlie,

I'm glad you've got a bed in the Royal Free Hospital and trust that it won't be too ghastly there. Life here is much the same. Your mother is in poorish form and apt to take it out on anyone who happens to be in her vicinity. Pongo is getting more and more doddery but his voracious appetite remains unimpaired. The other day he stole half a chicken mousse (your mother blamed and punished the unfortunate Moppet) and brought it up the following day on the carpet just as the Parkinsons arrived for lunch. We had dinner with the Surtees on Saturday and I sat next to a thin lady from Kensington who talked about death. The next day we lunched with the Thistlethwaytes which I much enjoyed. I slept in the car rather heavily on the way back. Peter Carew finished fifth at Sandown on a horse that appeared both unsound and unfit. Last Tuesday I had to go to a lunch in London and found myself at a table with Frank Chapple, head of the E.T.U [Electrical Trades Union], and a boozy left-wing MP called Russell Kerr, a tiresome right-wing Tory MP called Winterton, and the Editor of the Sunday Mirror. The poor little Home Secretary made a pathetic speech; it is hard not to despise him particularly as he is Welsh. The next day I went to a champagne and oyster party at Bentley's given by my bookmaker. I got cornered by two jolly surgeons who terrified me with talk about strokes. I hear Paul has had 'flu badly and one of Jane's sons has been poorly. Elizabeth Johnston, who lived at Eversley and used to photograph you and Louise, has had a ghastly operation at Windsor and I am anxious for her future. I had a letter from Cousin Caroline today; she is slowly recovering but is very weak still. I gather Audrey finds her neighbours in Basingstoke a pretty rough lot, mostly immigrants from East London. Your mother hasn't yet seen a house she likes. She is determined to drag me into some hunting country where I shall not know a soul and be bored to extinction. I suppose at my time of life it does not really matter; the main thing is to be near a cemetery. We are off to the Popes this afternoon. It is a good place to stay; excellent food, lots of bad vulgar jokes, no cards and early bed.

Well, best of luck and don't let the doctors bully you. They are apt to be conceited and dictatorial and don't like it all that much if you confer on them the status of garage-hands.

RM

I am briefly back in hospital for yet another liver biopsy under the care of the female equivalent of Sir Lancelot Spratt from

Doctor in the House. My father's advice on how to treat doctors is sound.

6 November

Dear Sir,

As your son Charlie delights in reminding me, I am rapidly approaching my mid-twenties whilst remaining unemployed. My father tends to agree.

I realise you are no longer fully involved in journalism but I am writing to you in the hope that you may be able to offer me some advice on how to rejoin the ranks on the staff of a reasonable newspaper.

Sorry to trouble you on so dreary a subject.

Yours sincerely,

Joe Gibbs

7 November

It might be more appropriate if you and I tried to find regular employment for Lupin Mortimer; who is now in his <u>late</u> twenties and whose activities seem to be of a somewhat irregular nature.

What do you call a 'reasonable' newspaper? What have you got to offer a 'reasonable' editor?

P.T.O.

Your background (Eton + distinguished military father) is against you. Most journalists are inverted snobs. Are you a union member? By all means come down here and talk to me about it. Frankly I am not optimistic about my ability to help: I have been out of the business too long.

RM

Do bring Joe down here one day though I doubt if my advice would be useful.

We have been asked to a party by Willie Carson and Dick Hern: fancy dress – we have to go as the name of a racehorse. Have you any ideas – not <u>too</u> vulgar or too expensive? Your mother's horse is lame so the atmosphere here is gloomy. Saw the Pirates of Penzance by the local school last night. Surprisingly good.

RM

My father is not exactly a connoisseur of fine music.

1980

Little Shiverings
Leaking
26 January

Dear Charlie,

I hope you are having a good time and that your health is improving. Life here is not entirely enjoyable thanks to appalling weather and a wide variety of strikes. I'm sure this nation has a death wish which may before long be fulfilled. There have been no trains from Basingstoke this week – two days of strikes and the lines iced up the remaining days. There is no food shortage anywhere but patients are having to leave hospitals because of the bloody-mindedness of the employees. Your mother had the time of her life today, being first on the scene at an accident near Kingsclere and therefore in an excellent position to boss the victims and apply first aid. We are off to the Surtees tonight – dinner for twenty in a shed! What price a touch of hypothermia? Your mother has a septic nose, a septic finger, a cracked elbow and an inflamed antrum but under the circumstances is remarkably cheerful. Your elder sister has been on holiday in Paris, presumably at the expense of Torday & Co. Unfortunately Paul's dog was run over and killed while they were away. He had cost £250 – a contrast to old Turpin who cost 7/6d. Aunt Joan is recovering well from her hip operation but has to be careful on the icy pavements. Not much news of Louise: I have not set eyes on HHH since that memorably disastrous Christmas party. At tonight's party I am sitting next to Lady Graham (née Susan Surtees). She can be rather sharp and I'm not sure whether she likes me. Surtees and I will have a party next June to celebrate having been friends for forty years. I first met him soon after becoming a POW and we were both really riding on the rims. He always swears the first thing I did was to swindle him out of a lettuce sandwich (we were on starvation rations); the second to teach him picquet and take off him what little money he possessed. I deny both charges. Tiny Man does not like the snow much and goes out as little as possible. Your mother is ordering a new car – another dreary old Renault. I met at dinner a year or so ago a man closely involved in a murder at Nairobi: in fact, I think he had pulled the trigger. I believe the atmosphere gets people rather overexcited out there. An old friend of mine, Dick Twining, died recently: he had played cricket for Eton in 1907 so was fairly old. An exceptionally nice and charming man.

Yours ever,

RM

I am in Kenya again, driving around in an old Land Rover earning my keep by doing odd jobs. I have managed to avoid a rather lively Christmas at home where my mother beat up my brother-in-law, HHH, following a row about flat racing. This particular Christmas came to be known as 'The Shining' with my dear mother playing the lead role of Jack.

Budds Farm
12 May

Dear Charles,

Two items of news: John Boyce died early this week. Could you represent the family at the Memorial Service? Secondly I see the Simmons factory in Newbury has been destroyed by fire.

I went to a very bizarre cocktail party in Boxgrove. A man I had never seen before asked me to come and meet his wife and himself. Unfortunately the wife was unable to be present, having decided to do a pineapple chunk! I hope never to see the husband again.

Yours ever,
RM

The retired headmaster of my preparatory school dies. My godfather, who once taught there, confided to me, 'He used to beat boys naked.' I said, 'Well he never beat me naked.' He replied, 'You were all right, you were family.'

Budds Farm
6 August

Did you read about Aunt Boo in the Sunday Express? She is described as an 'ex-actress'. I bet she contributed the paragraph herself. All quiet here but the geese crap all over the lawn. Your mother's dog is settling down well and the Cringer is like a mother to him. Your mother adopted three young hedgehogs all dripping with maggots and lice. Happily they have been transferred to the Bomers. The Derby winner Troy is coming to stand at the Highclere stud. They are trying to syndicate him for £7,000,000. Nick Gaselee won a race on the opening day of the jumping season.

RM

There isn't a political party in existence for which my mother's sister Aunt Boo didn't stand at one time or another. 'Keep Britain out of the Common Market' was a familiar theme, as was 'Keep Dorking White'.

Budds Farm
19 September

Dear Lupin,

I have not heard much news of you lately. What are you working at now (if anything)? Thank God our four geese were decapitated last week and not a day too soon. I hated them. Unfortunately Nidnod had allowed them too much

114

liberty and they weighed far less than expected. We ate the first one last night and it tasted like a moist flannel shirt. Not much local news: Serena Alexander is back home after a rather nasty operation. Colin Bomer told me that the annual communications bill for his firm was over £10,000. He must talk more on the telephone even than your mother. On Sunday we went to a champagne party with the Cottrills in the morning which I quite enjoyed. Mr C. is now seventy-three. In the evening we trudged off to the Darlings, drinks and then supper. It was all quite agreeable; as you might imagine the guests were a thoroughly respectable, dull collection of middle-aged members of the middle class so your mother and I fitted in well. Mr Randall has speared an unwary mole to death on the lawn and is very pleased with himself. Both the Surtees have had 'flu badly. Mrs S.'s son marries Miss Palmer on 5 October. All concerned rather hope he will treat himself to a wash and a shave prior to the nuptial ceremony. He has asked Major S. for an axe as a wedding present which strikes me as original. Your mother went off to Mrs Tweed's funeral today. I hear rumours that Hot Hand Henry is off on a trade trip to Italy.

How did you find Jane? What is her new house like? Has she managed to shoot anyone yet with her new gun? Mrs Wright is pushing the boat out and having a luxury swimming pool installed. Farmer Luckes treats the Bomers house as a convenient club and costs them a fair amount in John Haig. Mrs Luckes was seventy-nine on Monday. Several letters arrived for you this morning: they look to me like bills. Lord Carnarvon's horse irritated him by running extremely slowly in the St Leger. We had quite a lot of plums this year and I am getting a bit browned off with stewed plums for lunch and plum fool for supper.

Your affec. father,
RM

I am doing some odd jobs under the beady eye of my older sister in Northumberland. My mother's home-reared geese are clearly a huge culinary success.

Dear Lupin,

Thank you for your telegram which was greatly appreciated. I feel very old and doddery. Seventy-one is a ghastly age.

Yours ever,
Tightwad

In fact, almost any age for my dad was a nightmare.

Budds Farm
26 November

Dear Lupin,

I hear you have had influenza and are a bit seedy still. Your health is very important as if you are reasonably well you can just about cope with the inevitable asperities of life. Why not come here for a few days rest? Nidnod is devoted to you (appearances can be deceptive) and I enjoy your company even though your way of life is apt to be puzzling.

A warm welcome awaits you.

RM

The Leakings
Burghclere
Wednesday

Dear Lupin,

Not much squeak out of you lately. Are you all right? Life here is fairly normal. Your mother tried to annoy me by putting a dead rat on the kitchen table just as I was about to consume my usual hard-boiled egg but it really did not put me off all that much. Six inches of snow and a fearful blizzard. The herbaceous border crushed and our lovely laburnum tree broken off a few inches from ground level. No electricity for thirty-six hours. Your mother rashly invited the Bomers to lunch but unfortunately an emergency cooker blew up during the first course and nearly suffocated us with a nauseous gas that Himmler would have envied. Later that day the Bomers's black dog was killed by a lorry. Sarah was very upset. A man is here mending the burglar alarm and being a fearful nuisance. I shudder to think of the expense. Major Surtees is inspecting American vineyards in California; Mrs S. is in Holland with a lover. Their garden took a fearful battering the other day. No news of Louise though I wrote what I hoped was a tactful and conciliatory letter. On Monday we lunch with Lady D. On the whole I would sooner have a tooth out without gas. My horse was beaten by three inches at Wincanton so I shan't be able to buy a new hat after all. Today I try and sort out my tax affairs. I suppose financial simpletons like myself invariably get hotted both by the tax authorities and their own accountant. Did you enjoy Scotland? That country always make me think of 'Macbeth' and depresses me. The only time I enjoyed seeing 'Macbeth' was at Windsor where the old gentleman playing the title role was terribly pissed and kept on thinking he was King Lear. We get v. few invitations nowadays: as I am an aged and repetitive bore and your mother suffers from an incurable form of verbal diarrhoea, it is hardly surprising. The Surtees asked a local General and his wife to dinner. The General duly arrived but explained that's unfortunately his wife had been too drunk to get in the car! My old friend Desmond Brownlow has had his lovely statue of the famous greyhound 'Master McGrath' stolen from his garden.

Your affec. father,

RM

I am now having a go at 'knocking' on doors to buy antiques. I am told that I am not a natural. Lunch with my mother's oldest sister, Lady D., is clearly not one of the highlights of my father's life.

1981

Budds Farm

Dear Charlie,

Thank you for cleaning my quasi-suede shoes so well.
When you tire of your present employment, there could be a
future for you as a chauffeur-valet. Also thank you for
returning, after nine months, my snow boots. The fact that
one boot was deficient of a lace is of no account.

Yours ever,
RM

Budds Farm
9 January

My Dear Lupin,

All (fairly) quiet down here. Nidnod went to Dorset on Friday for the funeral of Dr Hollick who made a pass at her at the Portman Hunt Ball in 1938. In the evening she went to the Old Berks Hunt Ball with her boyfriend, Rodney Carrott, a portly, middle-aged insurance director, very rich and divorced from his wife who has been divorced again since. He has houses in Chelsea, the Isle of Wight and Corfu and drives around in a big BMW. He gave me a large bottle of Calvados and did not kick up a fuss when the Cringer made a mess in his room. The dance went off well and the next day Nidnod and the boyfriend went off for a ride on the Downs. Their pleasure was slightly marred by the boyfriend's horse dropping dead, I think from old age. It is a mistake to take a horse over twenty out of a sedate trot as the ticker is liable to pack up. I hope you like Rodney Carrott as he might be your stepfather once Camp Hopsons have wheeled me off to Swindon Crematorium. A friend of mine died in London last week. He fell and broke a leg in his flat and no one found him for thirty-six hours: by then it was too late. Aunt Boo is back from Israel: she departed madly pro-Jew and has returned fanatically pro-Arab! I hear Jane and her family have all been sick. Jane's cooking or a virus infection?

All the best,

D

Aunt Boo has a set of mahogany steps from which she holds forth most weeks at Speakers' Corner wearing a Jayne Mansfield-style nylon wig. Her political alliances are both numerous and various.

Budds Farm
24 January

Dear Charlie,

Is it true that you have achieved promotion? If so, I am indeed delighted and hope your success will be reflected in your wage packet. I trust life is not too awful for you; you ought to have some sort of fun at your age. Mrs Cameron came to lunch yesterday. She achieves the truly remarkable feat of talking more opinionated balls than even your dear mother. No wonder her husband declines to buy a hearing aid; it would not be to his advantage. Tonight I have to go to a Conservative meeting, the chairman at which will be Brigadier Eastman, who looks just like the German Commandant in the 'Colditz Story'. I am seeing Cousin Tom about your legacy on 8 February and will of course notify you of any development to your advantage, or otherwise. Your sister was twenty-four yesterday; she's getting quite an old bag. I met Captain Forsyth-Forrest yesterday. I gather his daughter has handed back her engagement ring to her ever-loving fiancé. They have decided that marriage is a waste of time and will continue to doss down together without the blessing of the Established Church. I have just sent an indelicate birthday card to Major Surtees; I hope it will please him and slightly shock his ball and chain. A heavy man with bobbed hair looking like a crooked Bishop in the reign of Henry VI came here to discuss burglar alarms. Nothing would surprise me less than to ascertain that he has done a bit of bird himself.

Your affec. father,

T. Tightwad (T.T.)

Any form of promotion for me is, indeed, unusual. Observations on my poor Danish godmother's ability to out-talk my mother is 'classic Dad'.

Budds Farm
Thursday

My Dear Lupin,

I have just forwarded to you a communication from Lloyds Bank. Would it not save time and trouble all round if you disclosed to Lloyds your London address? All v. quiet here. Nidnod is suffering from depression, quite common with ladies of her age and nothing to do with Beefeater gin. A lady from a London VAT office rang me up yesterday and was threatening in a distinctly offensive way. I told her I was just recovering from a stroke and if she caused me to have another my family would unquestionably take legal action. That caused her to adopt a slightly less hostile stance. The Randalls are in Scotland, having just returned from Blackpool. Their life consists of continual holiday on full pay. Major Surtees is due to make a speech at some big dinner and wants to know of a story rather vulgar but not downright disgusting as ladies will be present. If you can help, ring him at 01-636-3506. Mr Parkinson (D.F.) is unlucky; an elderly American-Jewess turned up on his doorstep demanding board and lodging TFO and claiming to be his geriatric mother-in-law's oldest friend. The Adams boys shot some pheasants yesterday; they have both passed into good colleges at Oxford [Christ Church and Magdalen] from a state school in Newbury. We had lunch at the White Hart with Sarah and Mark before the latter went to Oxford for his first term. The fried squid tasted like a very old bicycle tyre. Kate sent some photographs she took here. I look like something dug up for exhumation by Sir Bernard Spilsbury. Nidnod just looks wizened. Perhaps the camera can lie despite what is said to the contrary.

Keep working hard. I rely on you to keep me in my old age.
RM

Dad is an expert at debunking over-inflated egos and defusing zealous government officials.

14b Via Dolorosa
Burghclere

My Dear Lupin,

I have suddenly remembered it is your birthday on 4 April. I am unfortunately not in a position to give you a cheque for £1,000 as I am distinctly short of do-ray-mi at present so I fear you will have to make do with some smoked salmon which I have ordered to be sent to you. If my arithmetic is correct (it usually isn't) you will be entering your thirtieth year. It is an unlovely age: receding hair, shortness of breath, growing pomposity and in general a feeling that life has singularly failed to bring you your just rewards. However, cheer up! Forty is better as you then tend to give up caring, and accept the fact that in life's ranks you come into the category of 'also ran and made no show'. I think I became reconciled to that status during my second year at Eton and I have never seriously sought to improve it. Failures are usually more agreeable than the Lord Soames of life, and ambitious individuals are unhappy more often than not, being consumed by jealousy of any contemporary that shows signs of being a success. If there is any character in literature that I really admire it is Oblomov. If I had my life over again I think I would like to be a history don at a provincial university not far from the sea – long holidays with every excuse for reading, and during the term a chance to persecute any Marxist undergraduate with sandals, a beard and a proletarian accent. Recently a lady with a voice like the bottom of a gin bucket rang me up and asked me to write an article for Harpers & Queen. I have rashly accepted (am I now a sort of geriatric male Jennifer?) and I am going to be paid in liquor. Your mother is in v. poor form and very cross with everyone, particularly me. Louise seems to have broken off diplomatic relations with her so I don't visualise Hot Hand Henry coming down here for a year or two, and I think the Kennards can be erased from our Christmas Card list TFO. We stayed with Mrs Pope for Cheltenham: she was having a row with a horse-dealer who obliged by dropping down dead on the Thursday. We went to lunch with Rosie

Villiers who in a very nice way has lost most of her slates. She and her husband at intervals retire to the local asylum for running repairs and emerge a bit dottier than before. Captain Villiers is mad on hunting and politics and would like to impose the death penalty for a lot of not very serious offences such as nose-picking. Their son did himself in with drugs the other day. Lady de Mauley talked about the cost of temporary cooks while the Gold Cup was being run. Apparently she is known locally as 'The Duchess'. Miss Burnaby-Atkins (Rosamund) has got engaged to a twenty-year-old Belgian, a Roman Catholic whose parents speak not one word of English.

Your affec. father,
RM

It is my twenty-ninth birthday. My father's view of middle age is not altogether encouraging although, as it happens, it is pretty accurate.

Budds Farm
12 April

Dear Lupin,

I hope life in London is proving fairly agreeable. Your ingenuity in managing to exist without employment or receipt of what is vulgarly called 'the dole' is worthy of high commendation. Life here goes on in its usual bumpy rut. I was working in the garden last week and was disturbed by an exceptionally obnoxious smell. Bugger, I thought, it's those bloody drains again. However, I then found I was standing just by the corpse of one of the biggest rats I have ever seen. I gave it a decent burial, poor old fellow. Cousin Tom stayed here for two nights and I think enjoyed himself though he did say he had no idea your mother talked so much! We played bridge one evening and your mother played worse than anyone since bridge was invented. Mrs Anderson stayed here and kindly gave me a bottle of whisky: your mother got hold of it and I suppose I shall never see it again. Today, your mother has been participating in a 'sponsored' ride and for miles around people have been pestered to sponsor her. She swore the limit anyone would have to cough up if she completed the course would be £1. Luckily someone discovered in time that she had done her sums wrong and the sponsors would have each been stung for £175. I am doing an article for a truly ghastly magazine called 'Owners'. I only hope it will survive sufficiently long for me to receive payment. The editor (the magazine is printed in Eton High St) sent me a copy of the last edition which contains a long and somewhat unflattering article by John Welcome (nom de plume of an Irish solicitor called Burke) on the Merry family. I will keep it for you to read. Major Surtees had all his teeth out last week and his speech is a trifle blurred in consequence. Do you know any butlers or married couples willing to work in the country? Cousin Tom has no one – he is doing the cooking himself – and General Feilden is in a similar plight. Cousin Tom is now getting a flood of bills run up by his last butler, Blore, including one for four new tyres for Blore's car. When the local policeman was informed he said to Cousin Tom, 'I'm sorry, sir, but you'll have to take your place in the queue which is a very long one!' I believe Charles B. is making a fortune running the Arab connection for Hambros. Charles's ma-in-law is deposited at intervals in a dipsomaniac's home but always manages to escape which is very irritating for her near-and-dears. No news from Louise. Is Jane in Venice? Venice is nearly my favourite town. After the war I used to stay at the Royal Danieli for £1 a night. Marvellous food at Charley's Bar. A friend of mine married a Yugoslav refugee in Venice. Her relations smoked during the church service. No one is coming here for Easter. I look back with nostalgia to the days I used to buy you all Easter eggs at Southport when I was staying there for the Grand National. Colonel Draffen mutinied on his eightieth birthday and told his wife he was never again going to do anything he did not want to. Very sensible. Jeremy Aird backed out of his garage on Wednesday and ran over his wife's dog which has hardly augmented his domestic popularity. Augustus Barnett's shop at Wash Common has closed down which is a bore. I have just completed an article of quite unbelievable tedium about the Highclere Stud. However, I managed to include a paragraph about the way the Fifth Earl of Carnarvon used to dope his horses. I have more or less tamed a blackbird which comes and sits by me when I am gardening. It obviously thinks I am a complete bloody fool to work so hard. I saw Aunt Pam at Newbury; she is not exactly a sex kitten and makes things worse by wearing clothes purchased at Army charity bazaars and intended for the poorer families of other ranks. I hear Aunt Joan has done well on the Stock Exchange but she is a bit too crafty to admit it. She owns her flat which must be worth quite a bit.

Your affec. father,

RM

Just had the rates: £658. Scandalous. No wonder I have to lead the life of a genteel pauper.

Fortunately neither my father nor I can be accused of being over-ambitious and I guess surviving without being on the dole is something of an achievement in itself.

Budds Farm
26 May

My Dear Lupin,

I'm sorry to hear you are unwell. You have not looked particularly robust lately and I think you ought to have a check-up. After all, your health is the most important asset you possess. I think you ought to consider discarding the dusky witch-doctor you patronise and go to someone more rational. Our new doctor here seems quite adequate. Please get in touch with Mr Parkinson (95-700-257) who would like you to flog his car for him on a commission basis.

Yours ever,

RM

The new doctor alluded to is the bluntest I have ever met yet. Without a hint of irony he calls his house 'Bedside Manor'.

Budds Farm
6 October

My Dear Lupin,

I hope your health is holding out and that you are reasonably content at your new job. I have no idea what you do or where you do it. No doubt you will be appearing here in an expensive new motor before long. Your mother was hoping to have her first day's cubbing last Friday but it was cancelled as the head groom at the Old Berks stables had peppered a female employee with a humane killer and then blown his own head off. He had worked there for twenty-five years and the girl, whom Nidnod knew well, is thirty years younger than he was! It's odd the way demon sex keeps on obtruding into fox-hunting! Tim and Caroline Holland-Martin sold their yearlings well at Newmarket. They got 450,000 guineas for one and 20,000 guineas for another. Nice work if you can get it! Mrs Hislop is barmier than ever. Following a series of complaints, she was sent for by the stewards of the Jockey Club and told she would lose her badge (as wife of a Jockey Club member) if she did not behave herself in future. It was thought that the warning would cool her ardour but the next day she wrote a letter demanding a private dining room for women in the Jockey Club Rooms as the men were all so boring! The Gaselee stable had three winners on Saturday, 20/1, 16/1 and 3/1. The next day Mrs G. pranged her car which was a total write-off. Luckily she and her son were not badly hurt. King Chaos reigns supreme here as twenty-four people – mostly dull and elderly – come to lunch on Sunday. Harry Roper-Caldbeck left £1,250,000.

I believe Charlie Blackwell has returned to his wife. They

have been on holiday in Miami. Jane complains of being hard up: I have been told a great many times that Paul is a tycoon so she ought not to be wholly devoid of treacle. I shudder at the approach of Christmas. The alleged 'Festive Season' costs me about £350. I really wish I was a Non-Skid and spent 25 Dec at a kosher hotel in Margate. Nidnod met the Dingwalls at a funeral in Yateley last week. I have been sent the latest Dick Francis book; it is all about computers and I can't understand it. The Bomers are off to Brittany: not much fun at this time of the year, I imagine. A Burghclere woman has died of tetanus after scraping her arm on a bean pole. The new man at the Post Office is an improvement on the last one. There is a new Dr at Woolton Hill who looks like a retired jockey (may be one for all I know).

Your affec. father,

RM

How is that girl with the nice legs?

I am constantly amazed at how much entertaining news can be packed into a relatively short letter. My new job is with a property investment firm in London.

Budds Farm

10 November

Dear Lupin,

I hope all goes well with you. I have not seen your firm's name mentioned in any of the many criminal cases involving scrap-metal merchants. Not much news from here. We went to a rather ghastly dinner party, the guests being for the most part deaf old men and alcoholic old women. In addition there was an Old Etonian who had done quite a long term in prison, and a very fat lady who thinks Mr Parkinson murdered his third wife. On Sunday we lunched with Mrs Pope; among those present was Anthony Philippi whom I believe was concerned with your brief military career. Nidnod's horse has been unsound which has made her (Nidnod) a bit jumpy. I suppose I ought to go up to London and do some Christmas shopping but I simply cannot face it. I think I will make do with the Co-operative stores at Whitchurch. Smiths have opened a new premises in Newbury: you can buy almost anything there bar a book. My bedside lamp has disintegrated and I have been reluctantly compelled to replace it. I hear my cousin Mary paid £100,000 to her husband to go away. He has never been happier and is very rarely sober. A man came and cut all the hedges yesterday for £10: I would willingly have paid him twice that amount. On Saturday we go to old Geoff Barling's wedding: he is eighty. His previous wife went off her onion. The last time we saw her she clasped Nidnod to her bosom and started to sing 'Oh, You Beautiful Doll, You Great Big Beautiful Doll'. Nidnod tells me I was unkind to laugh.

Yours ever,
RM

Another new job – I am currently employed by a large scrap-metal company. This is my dream job especially as sometimes I get to drive the crane.

Budds Farm
24 November

Dear Lupin,

Thank you so much for your very generous present which I greatly appreciated. I'm so glad you were able to come to lunch. I met a man who worked in a big brewery the other day; 20 per cent of the draymen get sacked every year for dishonesty of some sort. I don't think your firm is unique.

Yours ever,
RM

Dad's seventy-second birthday. His view of my current employer is disparaging.

1982

Budds Farm
6 April

My Dear Lupin,

I trust you are in a moderately robust state of health and that your thirties will be happier and more successful than your past decade. I shall be relieved to hear (if ever) that you have found some little niche in the world of commerce as you have a longish wait still before the happy day arrives when you can stride boldly into the Post Office and draw your pension. Incidentally, Burghclere Post Office will soon be permitted to sell alcohol so I shall be able to purchase stamps, loo paper and claret simultaneously, a considerable convenience. Your mother is in very poor form and particularly cross because I warned her that Lord Carrington, one of her political heroes, would have to resign. She has been so boring about fox-hunting that I am considering a subscription to the local Hunt Saboteurs Association. No doubt you will be conscripted soon provided you pass the medical examination. Hot Hand Henry will probably end up in the Army Catering Corps. I am game to be RTO [Recruitment Training Officer] at Thatcham or Theale. There are lots of 'workmen' busy here so I foresee an avalanche of substantial bills in the not far distant future. Your mother is not indulging in entertainment to any marked extent over Easter but there is a faint possibility that the Bomers may come to lunch on Sunday. I went over to the Gaselees last night. Mrs G. plucky but weary with the house full of bolo children, fourteen of whom had sat down to breakfast that morning. Nick had influenza badly and looks very run down. The Cringer is fairly well but as deaf as a beetle. He spends most of the day asleep. I do not think he was responsible for the huge dead rat outside the stable: my own view is that Reg Rat expired from sheer old age and from that boredom with existence that inevitably overtakes the elderly. A sadly large number of shrubs and roses are dead on account of the cold weather in January and they have become very expensive to replace as well as an irksome fatigue to dig out and remove. Do you recollect the very sensible army maxim much used in the Coldstream in my day: 'It is infinitely preferable to incur a slight reprimand than to undergo an irksome fatigue'? Less popular were the words of an ambitious Aldershot general: 'The darker the night, the more inclement the weather, the better the exercise.'

Your affec. father,

RM

The Falkland's War has just begun. My birthday is always a good opportunity for a fairly bleak assessment of my general role in life to be issued.

Age Concern House

Dear Lupin,

Your sister is now in high esteem among her relations though I have heard nothing yet of your Aunt Pam's reaction, I hope she will follow it up with something equally successful. Journalism is a good deal more profitable nowadays than writing books which financially is just a waste of time. Journalists have always been disliked and despised but today their social status is slightly higher than it was in my youth when they entered a house by the back door and had to wait in the servants' hall! I hope you are enjoying your new job and you find it financially rewarding. My friend Paul Greenwood of Knight, Frank and Rutley has just been made redundant, a serious matter for a middle-aged man with children and a taste for fox-hunting. His wife can be a bit of a tartar which will hardly help his situation. On Friday we went to dinner at Chieveley with the Steels, who I like, not least because they have plenty of treacle. The dinner was revolting, the first course consisting of Lifebuoy soap. I sat next to an old bag called Lady Grimthorpe who annoyed me by feigning deafness. In my view she is an ideal candidate for the lethal chamber. Also there was Arthur Budgett who had a 33/1 winner at Ascot the following day. He certainly did not advise me to back it! At Ascot we had a very good lunch with John Abergavenny who is just retiring as H.M.'s Ascot representative. He is blessed with good looks and perfect manners and used to have a very beautiful sister who made an unhappy first marriage. His own son, the only one, died of cancer at Eton. John's successor at Ascot is Piers Bengough, a tough but agreeable South African Jew whose sister Mrs Quarry lived near the Thistlethwaytes at Eversley. I hope he will follow the example of Bernard Norfolk and John A. by letting us use the Ascot Authority stand throughout the year. At the party before lunch Mrs Beaumont introduced me to a little Polish girl whom I took to be twelve years of age. However, later I saw her with her noggin in a tankard of the hard stuff and with the other hand gripping a Gauloises, and investigation disclosed that she was twenty-six! At Cheltenham I saw a rather run-down elderly man, old in fact, and eventually realised it was Reggie Paget with whom I messed at Eton and whose career there was slightly less distinguished than my own. He is now Lord Paget and was for many years Labour MP for Northampton. He was also Master of the Pytchley. His father, a Tory MP, was killed out hunting and his brother became a bullfighter. He is the only Labour MP to have ridden round Aintree. His political career would have been more successful if he could have refrained from baiting Harold Wilson whom he rated an awful crook, no doubt rightly. He is a great admirer of Lady Salisbury and shares a racehorse with her. I think he is under the impression that she actually drives the juggernaut to Poland! Au fond Reggie, who is related to your mother, is a very kind person and I like him. There is a lot to do in the garden just now and Mr Randall has just announced his departure to Devonshire for a holiday. Mark Bomer has terrible acne, poor boy. He has amassed a wonderful collection of toadstools, some of a curiously erotic shape and size. Your mother is in fairish form but worries about twenty-seven different things. The poor old Cringer is fading way and this morning he just could not jump up on to my bed. Your mother is very patient with him and keeps him going.

1st lady: My dog did very well. He got a first, a second and was Highly Commended.

2nd lady: Mine did all right too. He had a fight, a fuck and was highly delighted.

Mrs Surtees has made her new house very attractive. I never see Major Surtees nowadays. The Cardens' horse won easily at Worcester on Saturday. No news of Louise or of HHH.

I loathe my new accountant, the Himmler of Reading.

Your affectionate father,

RM

I form an unlikely friendship with an elderly but delightful marchioness, Lady Salisbury, and together we embark on a Polish adventure delivering aid in a massive articulated truck which fortunately I have a licence to drive.

The Old Dank House

Dear Lupin,

I trust that your Polish trip went off well and there were no irksome misadventures. Jane rings up quite a lot: she seems well, but like most of us suffers from cashflow problems. I gather that Torday & Co are passing through an unprofitable phase. Your mother has a bad cold aggravated by riding for hours at a time in pouring rain. The garden looks like a picture of the Western Front in October 1917. I'm all for giving the people who fought in the Falklands full credit, but it is sometimes forgotten that in World War I it was not uncommon for an infantry battalion to lose twenty officers and over 400 other ranks in a single day. In the Falklands the infantry, thank God, were not asked to make frontal attacks through belts of uncut barbed wire against carefully sited and skilfully used machine guns. No news of Henry and Louise so I assume they have no worries. The Adams boys have shot several pheasants in the garden. I assume they (the pheasants) were either stationary or walking at a sedate pace. I was driving Nidnod to Newbury and she was very upset when she saw a dead pigeon in the road. She was just starting to give me a lecture on callous motorists when I pointed out that 'the pigeon' was in fact an extremely dirty towel. The Randalls have been down to Devonshire. They have a far jollier life than I do but they are probably better off. The Cringer is quite lively but a bit too nonchalant over where he lifts his leg. I hate my accountant more than ever: I have just caught him out telling lies, which of course has annoyed him a good deal. We have a lot of people turning up for lunch on Sunday which is rather a bore. Newbury races are 'off' as the course is under water. Jeffrey Bernard is staying at Kingsclere and I had a lot of expensive drinks with him at the Crown. I notice the death of J. H. L. Lambart, the last survivor of the Eton masters who had the hideous task of trying to teach me. He was John Surtees's House Tutor. Also Jeremy Thorpe's. Other masters called Lambart 'The Widow' because he was such an old woman!

Your affectionate father,
RM

I arrive in Warsaw on the day the Belgrano is sunk. Eager for my companion to inform her husband that she's OK, I suggest we use the telex at the British consulate to send the following message via my brother-in-law's company in Newcastle: 'Please call the Marquis of Salisbury and let him know that his wife has arrived safely.' He promptly calls a public house of the same name and leaves the message with a bemused landlord. On my return I am introduced to Jeffrey Bernard at the 'Lambourn Lurcher Show'. We are chatting away when a jolly, middle-aged lady bounces up and announces that she has just won first prize in the 'rough bitches' class.

Budds Farm
31 December

Dear Lupin,

Just a few words to thank you for your very generous Christmas present which was greatly appreciated. Your mother is in a very trying mood at present and you are fortunate not to be here! Cousin Tom is in a bad way although his mind is now clearer and he can speak a bit. A decision over the future will have to be taken soon. They may send him home with a couple of nurses and let him expire more or less quietly; or they may opt for another operation when he can stand it (not for two months) and which would cause a lot of pain and would carry no guarantee of success. It is all rather awful. Cousin John and Charles are seeing the top surgeon this weekend. The Cringer is quite well but being blind and deaf seems more stupid and obstinate than he really is. One just has to be very patient with the old boy. He can no longer jump on my bed (rather a relief for me) and he needs to be helped into a car. He and I both find old age rather ghastly! Mr Parkinson still has his mother-in-law with him. She downed an entire bottle of Scotch on Christmas afternoon. Simon is there temporarily. He says the Hong Kong Police Force, of which he is a member, is noted for corruption and homosexuality. The other day he barged into a little Chinaman carrying a suitcase which burst open tipping a lot of little packets on the pavement. Simon apologised and was helping to repack the case when the Chinese policeman he was with pointed out that the packets were probably drugs; as indeed they proved to be on investigation. Be fairly careful of Miss Cameron; she is good fun but mixed up with individuals who are apt to end up in the dock. Best of luck in 1983 and I hope you will continue to be gainfully employed.

Yours ever.

RM

1983

Budds Farm
28 January

Dear Lupin,

What an interminable month January is! Everyone is more or less ill and to some extent unhappy. Your mother is in her worst form and never stops complaining. I just keep my mouth shut and try and keep out of the way. I have booked for us to go to Crete in May. It will bankrupt me but at least it ought to be warm there. The Cringer is very senile and it is difficult sometimes not to get cross with him. I have an idea that certain people feel very much the same about me. Your mother is off to the opera (Rosenkavalier) with the Bomers tomorrow. I hope it will cheer her up a bit. I saw the Gaselees on Tuesday and drank far too much gin: I don't think my driving on the way home was above criticism. I have been asked to do some work for the Sunday Times colour supplement but I don't like the subject so I think I'll decline. At the end of the month I am going to see the shifty Bengali who does the accounts for 'Pacemaker' and I may have to put the frighteners on him. He owes me for five months. A girl of eighteen is coming to see me tomorrow about getting a job in the racing world. I am told she is good-looking which helps, but I don't rate her chances very high. I hear Jane's car was broken into and she lost a bit of kit. I broke a bottle of orange juice all over the front seat of my car this morning. A very nasty sticky mess! Aunt Pam is better but I gather Uncle Ken is feeling pretty ropey still. Your mother is in a fearful flap over the water and gets hysterical if anyone turns a tap on. I talked to Cousin Tom yesterday; he is making slow headway. He is better in the morning than after tea when he is apt to be terribly tired. I can't think of anything else to say.

Your v. depressed parent,

RM

Budds Farm

15 May

Dear Lupin,

I think you would be amused to hear I have been asked to appear in a radio programme called Down Your Way in which I would answer questions and then select a piece of music to be played. Alas, I shall be in Scotland and cannot oblige. I think I would have chosen something from HMS Pinafore or the Prize Song from Die Meistersinger.

Your mother insisted on giving Cringer some worm pills and he was hideously sick as a result.

Yours ever,

RM

The offer to become a minor celebrity is passed by.

Budds Farm

28 August

Dear Lupin,

V. dark and wintry here today. I may have to wear socks for the first time since June. I have just received a sweater (special offer) from a slightly bogus firm allegedly based on some remote Scottish Island. I think it is all right but rather unexciting, like most things from that part of the world. Baron Otto is settling down well; he is very affectionate and amusing. Peregrine hates him and has subsided into a permanent sulk. Major Surtees came to lunch yesterday on the way down to Somerset where he is trying to buy a house. He is taking twenty-seven pills a day prescribed by some quack doctor so not surprisingly he does not look particularly well. Mrs Burnaby-Atkins asked a lot after you when we went to dinner there. Also present was a former Governor of Nigeria with solid claims to be regarded as one of England's deadliest bores. I drank too much and told his wife two thoroughly unsuitable stories, one about a French letter. She did not give the big 'Ha! Ha!' We had a barbecue with the Bomers which went off reasonably well and no one actually caught pneumonia. Mr Parkinson is still having trouble with his mothers-in-law. Gaselee's stable were beaten in the final of the Lambourn tug-of-war competition (not very interesting but I'm short of news). Mrs Cameron comes to lunch tomorrow so I anticipate a fair amount of ear-bashing. This is Newbury Carnival Week – one of the most depressing functions in the whole of the year. Awful girls with dreadful acne riding in local commercial vehicles and claiming to be beauty queens! 'Funny' men in false noses being pushed in children's prams! Straggling processions of bolo brownies and snotty wolf cubs! Dreadful! The Randalls have a much better time than your mother and I do. I think they are off to Wales tomorrow. A brown hen has come to live in the garden. I rather like it and am making friendly overtures, so far repelled with hauteur. Some hens are a bit inclined to be snobbish. Are you taking part in the Notting Hill Carnival? I imagine a good many of your clients in that area will have converted kitchen utensils into instruments of percussion and will be making a hideous noise. Tough luck on people who went to Biarritz for a holiday and got drowned. My father used to like Biarritz, not least because my mother would not go there. He had a bird there, a fearsome old trout called Mrs O'Malley Keyes. During World War I, I was made to appear on the stage with her at a charity concert at the Wigmore Hall. My role was insignificant but my sense of embarrassment still lingers. I have never made my mark on the boards. Nor has my sister: we are both far too gauche. On the other hand Tom Blackwell sang the new boys song 'Five hundred fresh faces' at the Harrow School Concert, while his younger brother Charles obliged some years later with 'Dear Little Buttercup' from HMS Pinafore. I wrote a short play when in prison but it was not produced on the grounds that it was likely to cause grave offence. In fact, that had been the sole object of the exercise. I seem to have a dim recollection of a play got up by the Blackwell's governess, Miss Neighbour, in which Cousin John played the part, not all that successfully, of a mushroom. Pongo won the fancy-dress prize at the local dog-show in the guise of Sherlock Holmes. My mother once had a dwarf kitchen maid called Minnie who played jazz rather well on the piano. She was given the sack because her playing made the butler over-excited. In those happy days we had a chauffeur called Percy Samuel Woods who committed suicide by lying face downwards in a large puddle. Talk about doing things the hard way! I suppose we had some fairly weird servants, e.g. Kate Murphy who was pissed at a dinner party and fell face downwards in the soup; and a butler who had been wounded in the head in World War I and was apt to pursue Mrs Tanner, the cook, with a bread knife. To these could be added Brett who forged cheques: Ellis, who emptied the cellar and peed into the empty bottles; and Horwood who thought he had droit de seigneur in respect of the footmen.

Yours ever,

D

Dad recounts unusual stories about the goings on downstairs in his family home in Knightsbridge during the 1920s.

The Old Leaking Shack
Burghclere
11 October

Dear Lupin,

I enclose a Daily Telegraph cutting which might interest you. I have submitted a claim on the off chance of getting something. Whether I am entitled to anything I really don't know but it's worth having a go. The worst that can happen is a reply telling me to piss off. After settling my tax affairs this week I could do with a slice of cake. It is v. cold and wet here. Your mother has been busy decorating the church for a three-day flower festival and I must say she did her section very well. Needless to say some nosy old trout went and altered it which made Nidnod mad with rage. She went cubbing today and got frozen. However, she made friends with a rather tedious old colonel which cheered her up. I visited Major Surtees in his new office, a real tycoon's room with space for two billiard tables. I drank a lot of port and felt sick later but luckily wasn't. I have been busy doing a book review for the Times Literary Supplement, the assistant editor of which is Andrew Hislop. Tomorrow the Lemprière-Robins come to lunch: I intend to keep Mrs L-R. under strict control. Did you know Lillie Langtry's old dad was Dean of Jersey? He was known as 'The Dirty Dean' and sired a large number of illegitimate children. One man that Mrs Langtry used to bed down with was an oafish Scottish millionaire. After a row with a girlfriend he used to send as a present a tomcat with its throat cut! I heard a funny story about a peer who kept a private zoo. Not the Toad's father, I hope. I will tell you the story when I see you. It is about the peer's wife and a gorilla.

Yours ever,

RM

My mother tends to get 'dangerously excited' about fairly trivial matters. 'Crash helmets on, boys' is a familiar cry from my father when the calm of a quiet evening at home looks like it is about to take a sharp turn for the worse.

Budds Farm

22 November

My Dear Lupin,

Thank you so much for your card and kind message, both greatly appreciated. Frankly, I never expected to reach the age of seventy-four; still less did I anticipate a seventy-fourth birthday spent cleaning out the grate, washing-up saucepans and answering a disobliging communication from the Inland Revenue Authorities. Tonight I give a dinner for four at La Riviera; it won't be very good and there will be no change from £60. Unfortunately, as far as I am concerned, getting sloshed merely induces suicidal depression.

Your affectionate father,

RM

Birthdays were always an opportunity for my father to concentrate on the more positive things in life.

1984

Monday

My Dear Lupin,

How are things going with you? Are you (a) On the verge of becoming a millionaire? (b) On the brink of insolvency? (c) The subject of investigation by the Fraud Squad? (d) Or cruising along like me, in genteel poverty? Your mother went to concerts at Sydmonton on two nights. The cost was exorbitant, the food repellent. There was a debate on Unilateral Disarmament in which speakers included such dreary left-wing hacks as the Reverend Soper (whose daughter married Terence Blacker) and the Reverend P. Osterreicher. An inarticulate Conservative MP called Gummer led for the other side. Mrs Cameron stayed here on Saturday. She is worried about moving house and about Sandra's sudden marriage to a bucolic Australian. The happy pair are coming over here for a brief visit and there is to be a party in a fortnight's time. I gather the younger Cameron boy is having difficulties with the Jewish lady with whom he has been living for several years. She wants to marry him; he does not want to marry her; and her parents do not want her to marry a non-Jew. Lady de Mauley rang up last night: apparently Jamie's ever-loving wife has done a bunk and will not be returning. I do not know if another man is involved. Perhaps she got browned off living so close to Jamie's family. Baron Otto is settling down well. He has plenty of spirit and is not averse to biting anyone who annoys him. My horse looks well and I hope will run soon. Nidnod is in quite good form. She went to a gym class in Newbury the other day but, as I warned her, she is too old for that sort of lark and she will not repeat the experiment, I'm glad to say. Otto had a confrontation with a speckledy hen in the garden: the hen behaved with dignity and eventually saw Otto off. We have had bulldozers in removing the shrubs and the round patch of grass by the garage. It looks a bit better on the whole. I hear rumours of Aunt Pam knocking back the gin a bit during her visit to Jersey!

Your affectionate and disintegrating parent,
RM

A mixture of B and C would describe my situation fairly accurately. To quote from a letter to my older sister at the time: 'Your brother stayed the night and looked reasonably healthy. He arrived in the sort of Mercedes which usually conveys six Jewish bookmakers driven by a Cypriot chauffeur in dark glasses. By 1987 he will either be a millionaire in Peru or on the run from the police.'

14b Via Dolorosa
Burghclere

Dear Lupin,

I hope your cure, or whatever it is, progresses favourably. Has demon tedium raised its ugly head yet? We had a rather fatiguing weekend here with H-H Henry, Louise and Rebecca staying here as well as Emma plus Orlando, her very agreeable black husband who never spoke a word and found Nidnod's gabblings totally incomprehensible. (Who doesn't, if it comes to that?) On Sunday we had the Thistlethwaytes, Jane T. and Charlotte Blacker to lunch. Jane is very nice but rather prim and Emma tries to shock her! Charlotte is full of fun, wears rather odd clothes and works for the Conservative Party. The lunch party was a success and went on till 4.30 by which time I was committed to Egyptian PT. Nidnod had had her noggin in the bucket for a considerable period and was totally unplayable in the evening which enabled me to go to bed early and read peacefully. I have just finished a book by an ancient actress who described how her mother was kidnapped by relations and incarcerated at the Priory, Roehampton, at the time a well-known nuthouse. I have also read a book by Edward James whom I just remember at Eton where he looked eight years of age and was even more indolent than I was. He was in a better position to be indolent than I was since he inherited £1 million when he came of age, equivalent to £12 million today. People literally queued up for a chance of swindling him or robbing him. He married the dancer Tilly Losch, a very pretty Jewess who, en deuxième noce, became Lady Carnarvon. I don't know why James married her as he greatly preferred men, in which respect he resembled the hideous actor Charles Laughton who was a natural for the Hunchback of Notre Dame. I have been recommended a book by Hallam Tennyson, an Old Etonian Marxist Homo who goes in for rough trade and is constantly getting beaten up by skinhead lovers. Major Surtees called in on Saturday. He has more or less bought a house in Wiltshire with good fishing. He left us a delicious trout. I know nothing of Jane: she has given up answering letters, a habit now contracted, I'm sorry to say, by her elder son. (For God's sake, don't mention that to Jane or she'll murder me.) Batten, a solicitor, lunches here tomorrow: I'd better lock up anything of value. Did you read about land-development at Hook in either the Sunday Times or the Sunday Telegraph? The Darlings are in Normandy for some beano.

Yours ever,
RM

P.S. Nidnod had written down the wrong day and at 6 p.m. a man suddenly arrived to see the house and was shown round by Nidnod wearing an ancient and very tight bathing dress bulging dangerously at inconvenient places. He proved to be a merchant banker (rich?), very good-looking, charming, half Peruvian, half Swedish. He is a member of the Turf Club, has had relations at Daneshill and Tudor Hall, and has a son at Ludgrove. I doubt if he was much interested in the house but we all got on very well though it was seldom that he or I managed to get a word in! The Bomers have killed off their wretched old dog and are getting a new one. A mistake, in my opinion.

Dad indulges in a spot of Egyptian PT (military slang for forty winks). Finally, I succumb to the inevitable and book into a drink and drug rehabilitation centre in Weston-super-Mare. I throw my empty brandy glass out of the open sunroof as I drive through the entrance gates.

I hope you like your school-mates and are not getting a bad time in the dormitory. Is the tone of the school good? No dirty talk I trust. Your mother is coming down on parents' day.

   D

When Dad comes down to visit me we go for a walk on the beach where he says, 'It seems very pleasant here, old boy, but what exactly are you here for?' 'Oh, I've just got a bit of a drink and drug problem.' He thinks for a moment before responding, 'Any chance of getting your mother in?'

The Crumblings
Burghclere

Dear Lupin,

   Some people called Prentice have just rolled up in a BMW to inspect the house: American, young, well-mannered but not the least interested and better suited to Virginia Water or Ascot. I hear you have been made a prefect; can you wear a tassel on your cap and are you permitted to cane 'difficult' girls? We went to the

Derby and got there in ninety minutes. We had badges for the Directors Stand and had a marvellous view. Lots of posh people there and Nidnod thought Willy Whitelaw was the caterer. During the race I stood next to an awful female trainer called Jenny Pitman. She remembered I had once written that I would 'not walk a mile in tight boots to have a drink with her' and accordingly cut me dead. What a cow! The owner of Secreto left Italy in a hurry and has made a fortune in Venezuela running buses. Accountant Kiely came to lunch yesterday and told us all about a rather peculiar operation he once had. Nidnod now thinks he's wonderful. Earlier in the week Batten lunched here and soon afterwards sent Nidnod a large bill. Colin keeps dropping in for money and the bank has lent me a huge sum that I don't suppose I shall ever be able to pay back. Mr Gluckstein (of Salmon & Gluckstein) comes to see the house tomorrow. At least he has a rich name. Nancy McLaren has bought the Gosling's house at Inkpen. Grazebrooks and Parkinsons to lunch tomorrow. Otto is very randy and is happy to make do with his own sex. I feel increasingly old and weary; I may have to contact Mr Kiely's in-laws who are successful undertakers. Lady Hadow had to have her dog put down yesterday – a growth on the liver. I bought some strawberries yesterday: v. expensive and tasted of cardboard. Stick to bananas, I say. Mrs Alexander has flown to Australia as her mother is v. ill. Mr Kiely went to Hove to see his dying mother who is ninety-one. He told the doctor to 'make her comfortable' which I suppose meant 'put her down'. Two days later she had sausages and bacon for breakfast and was reading the Daily Mail. I rely on you to help Nidnod move if I fail to stay the course.

Your affec. father,

RM

I am now effectively head boy of a substance treatment centre. This is no mean achievement in my opinion and an all-time first to be head of anything.

Budds Farm
Monday

My Dear Lupin,

By the way, did you know that the original Lupin is buried in Highgate Cemetery close to Karl Marx? How are you getting on at Weston-super-Mare? I hope the treatment is not too ghastly and that you feel it is doing you good. At least you possess a sense of the absurd (something not possessed by Nidnod or Mrs Thatcher) to help you bear the less tolerable aspects. What is the food like and does sex ever rear its hideous head? Your mother enjoyed her visit but returned in a ferocious temper and put me through the mangle in no uncertain fashion. In those moods she is very like Mrs McClintick in 'Casanova's Chinese Restaurant' by Anthony Powell. (Mr McClintick eventually gassed himself in Vauxhall.) I hope you will be out in time to give a hand with the move to Kintbury. Frankly I dread it. I wish I was fifteen years younger. Unfortunately I am rapidly becoming senile and my general health is deteriorating rather fast. Old age is full of surprises, most of them unpleasant, and is rather like being punished for a crime one has never committed. I dread another winter; we seem to be heading for one rather fast without even a glimmer of summer yet. We keep the same doctors at Kintbury: better the devil you know, etc.,

etc. My inside is giving me hell at present but if I go to surgery for some soothing medicine I shall be whipped off to hospital, deprived of the last tattered shreds of human dignity, and tubes will be inserted into every orifice that I possess. The biggest mistake I ever made was to come round after passing out when buying cut-price gin in Newbury. I have hardly had a day's health or happiness since. I suppose very few people are ever really happy. The most one can hope for is to be reasonably content; and precious few people achieve that. Sarah-Jane Parkinson developed acute appendicitis in the middle of the night and was whipped off to Battle Hospital. She is OK again now. Desmond's mothers-in-law continue to be a problem. Aunty Vi is totally gaga and does not know who she is or who anyone else is either. From time to time she pours hot Ovaltine over the heads of her attendants. Paddy's mother is back with Desmond, probably for good. She does in a bottle of John Haig per day and tops up with a helping of Beefeater gin. My godson Johnny is in a Buddhist monastery and cannot communicate with the outside world for three-and-a-half years. I don't think he is missing much. By the way, would you like me to visit you? I could come down in my new car and stay at a hotel. Probably the staff at your place would take one look at me and shove me in a padded cell. I like my new car but must try and find out what all the knobs and switches are for. I want to discover how to turn the heater off before the weather gets hot. I had lunch with Mrs Surtees yesterday (partridge, blackberry tart). She is working two days a week in a shop in Hungerford. I believe Major Surtees has bought a house near Wilton, Wilts. Tonight Nidnod and I have supper at The Miller's House with Sir Michael and Lady Hadow. Sir M. is outwardly the smooth

Foreign Office type but in fact is a Grammar School Boy (Berkhamstead, where Graham Greene's father was Head Beak) and was originally in the Indian Civil Service. He transferred after Indian independence to the F.O. and did well in Paris and Moscow. His last two jobs were Ambassador in Israel and Argentina. I think he has had previous wives. Lady H. is a plump Jewess with a strong East End accent. She was formerly in the antique business and was married to a Mr Sieff of Marks and Spencer and Ashford Hill. I rather like her. God knows how I am going to pay for the house with shares rushing downhill like the Gadarene swine, the coal strike, the war in the Middle East and the unpredictable antics of President Reagan. I think I shall be bankrupt by August. I enjoyed my trip to Brighton: I would give my eyes to be retiring to a flat there with a nice view of the sea and the nudist beach. Cousin John is recovering from his nasty fall. I hear that the income of my chum Khalid Abdulla is just over £1 million a day. Nice work if you can get it! The Hislops are asking £750,000 for their place. They may be a bit short of treacle as Brigadier Gerard shows signs of becoming sterile. Charlie Blackwell wants to marry a Miss Birkbeck from Norfolk. The Langham Stud is being let for seven years. Charlie is leaving Hambros to work on his own; he intends to live at Langham. Caroline and Tim lost all their silver when burglars raided Overbury. They were in bed at the time and heard nothing; nor did the dogs. Otto behaved vilely when I took him to lunch with Mrs S. He peed on the carpet and tried to do his mother and his aunts. Have you read a book called 'The Diary of Adrian Mole'? I rather enjoyed it. I must go and have the hard-boiled egg and slice of rubbery bread that constitutes my breakfast.

Keep in touch and ring me up,
Your affec. father,
RM

*A potential new home is identified in the village of Kintbury.
My father confides that in seventeen years at Budds Farm he
never spent a happy twenty minutes there. However, my
mother, despite agreeing to the move, takes great exception
to Kintbury, which she promptly christens 'Cuntbury'.*

Budds Farm
17 July

Dear Lupin,

The day set for our move fast approaches and there is no
shortage of problems and worries. As you know it is a smaller
house than Budds Farm, four bedrooms as opposed to six.
The question is: what do you want done with all your
manifold possessions here? There is more junk in your room
than there are maggots in a dead crow. Stacks of old magazines, school books, mementoes, etc. To say nothing of
clothes, pictures, etc. The ideal solution would be for you to
organise a move of all your 'lares et penates' to your place of
abode in London: and to dispose of all the junk you no longer
require. I could, rather unwillingly, store some of your things
in one of the outhouses at Kintbury but there is no room for
them in the house. Louise is having to move her things, too,
but as the owner of two houses she really has no problem.

My lovely clothes cupboard was flogged to a dealer in Camberley and I'm living out of suitcases. During the dismantling of the cupboard, my pearl tiepin vanished!

I feel sure we can come to an amicable arrangement about your belongings. I don't want to make difficulties for you but I don't want to fill the new house with motoring magazines of the 1950s.

Yours ever,

RM

I am not exactly obsessed by cleanliness and tidiness. To quote from a letter from my dad to my younger sister, 'Your dear little brother is coming home today so I expect my bathroom to become a mass of grime, dirty clothes and filthy bits of sticking plaster.'

Budds Farm

13 August

Dear Lupin,

Does Mr Varey sort out your tax problems? He is very ill in hospital after two heart attacks.

I am enduring a lot of agro from a female tax inspector at Andover who is doing her best to see that I become insolvent.

My eye is troublesome still; also various other organs and limbs. I am falling to bits like a 1929 Morris-Cowley.

Your affec. father,

RM

*I didn't have any tax problems because I had (at that time)
never knowingly paid any tax.*

The Miller's House
Much Grinding in the Marsh
5 November

Dear Lupin,

As you can doubtless observe I have bought a new type-writer. It is Japanese, cheap and extremely nasty. I already dislike it very much indeed. Yesterday we drove to Odiham for Nancy Campbell's seventieth birthday. Excellent food but not overexciting as I was one of the younger guests: all the women looked like Bank Managers' widows from Haslemere. Uncle Ken complained about his eyesight but eventually fluffed to the fact that he was wearing two pairs of glasses! He and Aunt Pam are wintering in Australia. I was inoculated against 'flu today by the district nurse who might have been Crippen's sister. Tomorrow we go for drinks with a plump lady whom I much dislike, and on Thursday I attend my first meeting as a Committee member of the Animal Health Trust. On Friday we go to the Mayhew-Sanders box at Cheltenham where I hope the browsing and sluicing will be of a high order. On Saturday old Weavers Loom is scheduled to run at Windsor. I'm glad I'm not in India; the locals can get very spiteful, particularly the Bengalis. What odds will you give me about the Queen and Mrs Thatcher both being alive on 25 December 1985? Cousin

John is off on a golfing holiday in Barbados. Charles B. wants to marry again but so far no divorce. I see 'Private Eye' is threatening to reveal something murky about Chapman Pincher when he was serving in the RASC, commonly known as 'Ally Sloper's Cavalry'. Mrs Hislop's mother cooled last week; she was a compulsive gambler. Nancy McLaren has sold her house to Susan Hampshire, now married to a rich Greek.

Look after yourself,
RM

The new home, with both village newsagent and surgery within easy walking distance, perks Dad up a bit, whereas the new typewriter is not a big hit.

The Miller's House
26 November

Dear Lupin,
We went to Bath on Thursday. Non-stop rain. After lunch Nidnod could not find where she had parked the car. En route we had drinks at the Pack Horse at Chippenham kept by a Coldstreamer who joined in 1932 as a boy of fourteen. He had been burgled two days after his guard-dog had been run over.

V. good lunch with Denise on Sunday: excellent roast beef; a rather 'difficult' daughter. Saw myself on TV, an experience that removed for good any lingering shreds of self-esteem. Denise played Bach on the clarinet. She is not as good as Mr Parkinson. I went to 'Pacemaker' to draw some money. Found the Bengali accountant had been sacked and the accounts department in utter turmoil. No record of my having ever done any work! I said I thought I was owed £540 and they paid up without any argument: I wish I had asked for more. I sent £5,000 to the Inland Revenue; I suppose that is mere canary seed to the Boltons set! Pinched the Post Office pen by mistake this morning. Mrs Surtees gave me a weird book for my birthday called 'Empire in the Sun'. I suppose a pretty good book, very original, but I felt a bit sick at times. All about a boy of eleven (English) captured by the Nips at Shanghai in 1941. Nidnod is in London. I have been looking after the dogs who have driven me more or less bonkers. There are times when I wish the sandy Tom who comes into our garden would eat the pair of them. Chaos at Newbury races on Saturday when the car-parking got out of control. Some savage fights took place. I found a pitch in a corner reserved for limbless racegoers. I'm reading an excellent book on the Civil War by a man with the unusual name of Windham Ketton-Cremer. I came across a man called Trampleasure the other day.

Your affec. father,

RM

P.S. Have received v. satisfactory special offer jersey from the Isle of Skye. On Wed John Oaksey comes here as he needs help over a book. I can tell him about the subject of the squaddie getting clap in 1933. Perhaps not very suitable for inclusion.

Nobody could accuse my father of possessing an over-inflated ego.

1985

The Miller's House
17 January

Dear Lupin,
    I hope you are in reasonable health and are profitably engaged in flogging property in the area of Notting Hill Gate to natives of one shade or another. V. cold here but this house is much warmer than Budds where the pipes are frozen and they have no water, hot or cold. Nidnod is well bar insomnia but recuperates with Egyptian PT from 2 p.m. till 5. The man with whom our cousin Mary was living was found dead in a copse: ticker trouble. An old Army friend, General Coxwell-Rogers, died last week. Widely known as 'the chap who was never ragged about his name at school'. Also dead was my former commanding officer General Sir Guy Salisbury-Jones, whom we called Winchester-Smith. I remember an officer called Wyllie-Rodger whose nickname was 'Cunning Fucker', while a rather boring man in a Scottish regiment called

Grant-Peterkin was referred to as 'Giant Foreskin'. Louise seems to have moved into her new house unimpeded by the fact that the previous occupants had omitted to move out. Hot Hand Henry has recovered from influenza. Major Surtees is having trouble with his new house and has not moved in yet. Lord Clanwilliam, a friend for fifty years, comes to lunch this week. He longed to have a son but Lady C. presented him with seven daughters! Their lovely house in N. Ireland was recently burnt by the IRA. When a penniless young officer, Gilly (as he was known) bought the biggest Bentley I have ever seen from a garage in Brookwood. He drove me up to London. We filled the tank at Brookwood and had to refill it at Staines, rather an expensive vehicle. I lent Gilly my Vauxhall in Egypt and he lost it. Luckily he came into a lot of money and married a rich and very amusing wife. I have bought a new mower, a Hayter, and a new sofa from that shop by the Post Office in Eton. Otto hates the cold and is fairly nonchalant about where he deposits his manure in the house. Peregrine is worse in that his messes are larger. I apologise for this writing paper: I have 5,000 sheets and must get rid of it. I am giving Nidnod and two friends lunch at the Dundas Arms on her birthday. That might set me back £100! I have just bought two paperbacks by P. D. James. I think she is the best modern writer of murder stories. I have to go up to London on the 5th for a lunch at the Hyde Park Hotel. Last year I sat next to the trade union leader Frank Chapple who is a gypsy, an ex-communist and now Scargill's bitterest enemy. A brave and entertaining man who exposed the communist conspiracy within the ETU. I see Lord Birkenhead died playing real tennis at Oxford. I knew his father at Eton who died quite young. The 1st Lord Birkenhead, the great Lord Chancellor, was an unscrupulous scoundrel from Liverpool who had a superb legal brain and a gift for invective. He had fearful rows with judges when he was plain Mr Smith. Once a judge observed to him, 'Mr Smith, you are being extremely offensive,' to which Smith saucily replied: 'As a matter of fact we both are. The difference is that I'm trying to be and you can't help it.' He made a brilliant maiden speech in the House of Commons that rallied the stricken Conservatives after their ghastly defeat by the Liberals in 1906. He was Winston Churchill's greatest friend; au fond, they were both political adventurers with a touch of the cad. Birkenhead died of drink in his fifties.

D

P.S. Had lunch with Dick Ker last week. His son, whom you knew at Eton, runs a gallery in Bourne St. SW. I want you to take a picture there for valuation.

Now thirty-three, I manage, at last, to acquire my first home in the form of a one-bedroom flat overlooking Parsons Green. A month or so later, my mother visits me and is appalled to discover that I have no hoover, no fridge and, most significantly (at that precise moment), no lavatory paper.

1986

Dear Charlie,

Very chilly here and not a sign of rain. The garden is like the Gobi Desert. Lunched yesterday with Gilly Clanwilliam who is handing over the big house to one of his six married daughters and is moving into a cottage on the estate. Lunched the day before with the Gaselees. Two of Mrs Pitman's lads pinched their posh Audi and vandalised it. The Edgedales are lunching here today. I'm still alive but not offensively so. At least I sleep well but all food tastes like iron filings.

xD

The Miller's House
15 January

Dear Lupin,

I hope you had a good time in North Africa. Did you have

to doss down in some Arab dive full of black men with foot-rot? However, you seem to have survived. I have just finished writing an article titled 'First Impressions of Kintbury' for the parish magazine. In the improbable event of anyone reading it, I anticipate a few bricks through the double glazing at The Miller's House, the first thrower being the vicar, the Revd J. H. D. Forklift MA. I have been quite busy with committee meetings for the Animal Health Trust, arranging a visitors' day at the Highclere Stud with refreshments (plonk and petit beurre biscuits). I am too impatient to be a good committee-man and am not very adept at concealing boredom, possibly, from lack of practice. Things are a bit dodgy at Highclere as owing to all the shooting there, they are being persecuted by the PLF (Pheasants Liberation Front). I had a bad day last Wednesday. Otto wanted to be let out at 6.55 a.m. I let him out of the front door and he at once bolted for the road through the garden gate which had been left open. Game to the last, and it nearly was 'the last' too, I pursued him in my pyjamas, dressing gown and slippers. Unfortunately I slipped on ice and fell heavily. The ground was so slippery that I could not get up and it looked as if Demon Hypothermia was going to get me, Nidnod being in London. However, I took my shoes off as I slipped less in bare feet, and eventually got back to base despite two more falls. I then got a stick, different shoes and went out again, eventually rounding up the culprit. After coffee and whisky, followed by a hot bath, I began to thaw but felt very old and shaken for three days afterwards. The Van Straubenzees came to lunch on Sunday and I mixed a powerful cocktail using plenty of coarse Spanish brandy. Nidnod's red wig tilted to an increasingly jaunty angle and she never stopped talking complete balls for a single second. Miss Gaselee evaded her ever-loving parents the other day and had her hair dyed purple for a party. Her parents were not noticeably pleased. I have managed to get a very good, rather rare book on the Phoenix Park Murders (the Irish carved up Lord Frederick Cavendish and the Chief Secretary with surgical knives outside Viceregal Lodge). Luckily the assassins ran true to Irish form and there was no lack of informers. I have just bought a load of logs which I now find are green and damp. Peregrine spends his whole time doing Otto and both dogs are in a condition of exhaustion by teatime. The accident of sex makes little difference to the love affairs of members of the brute creation.

Two definitions of a Gentleman:

1. He has all the qualities of a saint bar saintliness (Hugh Kingsmill).

2. He always gets out of the bath to do a pee (Anon).

The Government seem to be in a mess. This country is full of intelligent Jews. Why, therefore, must Mrs Thatcher employ three really stupid ones in Lawson, Britton and Joseph? To be fair, Joseph isn't stupid; he's barmy.

A man died the other day who figured in a typical Eton legend of the 1920s. Apparently his tutor, an old booby called Crace, caught him red-handed (hardly the appropriate expression)* after lights out with a colleague, and started to kick up a fuss. The criminal kept his head and observed to his tutor, 'Don't take it too much to heart, sir. You must realise I'm going through a very difficult phase.'

Your affec. father,

RM

*Crace was later heard to say to another beak, 'I found two boys in a very strange physical position which they were at a loss to explain so I'm afraid they will have to go.'

I have just returned from several weeks travelling round Morocco. Dad's contribution to the parish magazine is along the lines of 'Six easy ways to die whilst gardening'. He is not asked to write any further contributions, which was perhaps his plan in the first place.

The Miller's House

Dear Lupin,

I so sorry to hear you are poorly and I wish you a speedy recovery. I see the Duke of Norfolk has had a stroke on a hot day while in Morocco: it does not sound a very healthy place! I hope your hospital is competent; let me know if there is anything you want or if I can help in any way. I think I remember the hospital: I used to pass it seventy years ago on my way to a walk with Mabel in Battersea Park. Last night Sir Frederick Corfield QC stayed here. He is a Crown Court judge at Reading. During the war he was my partner with the radio in prison. He is very chatty and quite out-talked Nidnod, even at breakfast! I wrote to the Hotel Metropole in the south of France for rooms (demi-pension) for Nidnod, myself and Jane for a week in May. They demanded £350 a day which was a bit steep and I told them to stuff it. I then tried a hotel at Les Baux but that was full up. I am now trying a small hotel at Joucas which the Bomers liked.

Hideous weather and the dogs prefer peeing indoors. I hear you have got some spots. Our family is addicted to rashes – Nidnod came out with one the day before she was married – and I think it is because we are all highly strung. Headaches are another family weakness and in 1935 I had one after a migraine that lasted for a year before suddenly disappearing when I backed a good winner at Ascot. I had another apparently permanent headache after the war and went to see Dr Desmond Curran, the top neurologist who thought I had a brain tumour or was mad. He told me some good stories about criminals he had examined. Perhaps we are not a very healthy family: the only time I have felt really well was at school and in prison. On the other hand my father was never ill between the time he left Marlborough and his death at the age of seventy-eight. Nidnod is cooking very badly and dishes up some really terrifying mush!

My sincere good wishes for a speedy recovery,
RM

I end up in hospital with a hideous rash.

20 February

Glad to see you looking reasonably healthy. Don't work too hard: most tycoons have their first heart attack before they are forty! More snow last night.

I have no sympathy for those rich twits who forked out money to a con man who offered to get rid of Satan. I see an ex-Eton Master (now at Radley) has been found dead in weird circumstances. Thank you very much for the lunch.

RM

Feeling better, I buy an old Mercedes, drive down to Kintbury and take the old folks out for lunch.

30 March

Are you still 'in property' or are you an antiquarian book-seller? If the former please note that the McCalls are flogging their Windlesham house and want to buy one in London in the good old SW area.

4 bedrooms, small garden, convenient car-parking.

Price £310,000. Can you help?

D

P.T.O.

Nidnod has smashed up my car: it will cost hundreds to repair!

I am having another rapid career change.

1987

The Miller's House
16 July

Dear Lupin,

It was very nice seeing you and I hope you will come down again soon, not necessarily in a bread van. I trust your partner has recovered from diarrhoea as apart from the sordid discomfort it is not an easy word to spell. Have you sold any pants yet? With those samples carried in a bag, you look a proper commercial traveller (sales representative?). Aunt Joan has been told by Cousin John that she is very well-off indeed for a single woman and he is making her spend £10,000 on flat improvements, including decent heating. I have no idea who her heir is! I wrote to Cazenoves last week asking to be told the state of my marriage settlement. I was mildly surprised when a Mr Pascoe wrote back and said the settlement did not exist, having been wound up some years ago! This shook me somewhat but I was convinced Pascoe was talking balls. I rang up Cousin John who contacted Cazenoves and found someone had bogged it. In fact, the settlement now stands at £160,000 and I don't wish it to disappear although it may be a trifling amount judged by Cazenoves' standards. I have written to Pascoe suggesting some digital extraction on his part! Sarah Bomer came to lunch in v. good form. William has passed his law exams.

Your affectionate father,

RM

P.S. I hear Jane has given up her proposed trip to France. Two people killed at Greenham last night.

A Greek friend and I start a company manufacturing boxer shorts in Asia. We call it Raffateer Boxer Shorts: 'Are the boxer shorts in your life as exciting as the life in your boxer shorts?'

The Miller's House

18 November

My Dear Lupin,

Nidnod has just gone off to the opening meet of the Old Berks so I am having a quiet morning at my desk trying to deal with communications from my stockbroker and my accountant. No good news ever comes in a buff envelope.

J. Atkinson Grimshaw is one of my favourite artists. He is having an exhibition in Dover Street. If you have time, look in and see if there is anything I could invest in (£2,000). I might just as well have a picture as keep the money tucked away in a provincial building society.

Nidnod has a sore toe which makes her crusty. Her old boyfriend Rodney Carrott came to lunch yesterday. Tomorrow we go to the B-Atkins' beano.

Yours ever,
RM

I am in full agreement here. No good news comes in a manila envelope.

1988

Monday

Dear Lupin,

We lunched with the de Mauleys yesterday. I sat next to a plainish lady who works for the Evening Standard and used to share an office with Bristow. She likes him but he is a hopeless alcoholic.

Jane's elderly boyfriend has been poorly (ulcer). I hope he's not cracking up already. The Carews were here for the weekend. Benjamin was not on his best behaviour. Louise likes her German G.P.

Gordon Richards was no womanizer and after losing his virginity rather late in life he summed up the situation as follows: 'If that's cunt, I don't much like it.' Desmond Parkinson is back in hospital with a haemorrhage after a painful nose operation.

Dad always seems to have a bottomless pit of mildly inappropriate stories concerning characters from the world of horse-racing.

5 April

My Dear Lupin,

Congratulations on reaching the age of thirty-six. You have now got to contend with receding hairlines, deteriorating eyesight, diminishing ability to attract the opposite sex and a stomach that causes your tailor to make sarcastic comments. I have sent you a small present but it may not reach you and you have yet to favour me with your current address. We have had a quiet Easter here. Francis Reed out-talked your mother but made up for it by giving us all lunch at Great Shefford, mowing the lawn and mending the Hoover. The lunch was only slightly tarnished by having a table of overweight lesbians about eighteen inches away. One looked like a grossly inflated toad; another reminded me of a female all-in wrestler I saw battling away in a huge bowl of fish in 1928. We had a lunch party at home which went off reasonably well and a drinks party where some of the guests showed signs of wishing to camp down for the night. Drinks with the Parkinsons: Johnny, released from a Buddhist monastery, is now looking after the Dalai Lama! I do have some weird godchildren.

D

Another birthday and Dad weighs in with all the negatives he can muster. If I am asked my occupation, I simply respond that I'm a middle-aged, middle-class spiv.

1989

10 February

Dear Lupin,

Nidnod seems v. pleased with her sporty new car. A statement to my insurance company by a 'neutral' party came down firmly on the other side. I always thought this would happen but did not dare say so! I wonder what Nidnod will say!

D

My dear mother tends to navigate the roads with the same gusto and competitiveness that she deploys on the hunting field.

10 March

Dear Lupin,

I suggest you contact Cousin John and go and look at the Blackwell property, Copse Farm near Hatch End, Middlesex. If planning permission could be obtained, it would be worth £40,000,000; without it, only £500,000.

My dear old grandfather Thomas Blackwell, an old-fashioned liberal and wholesale grocer, owned a lot of land round there. He gave away land for Grimsdyke Golf Club, Oxhey Golf Club, Stanmore Golf Club and I think Sandy Lodge Golf Club! He also gave the land for the Commercial Travellers School and gave to the school a mass of Victorian paintings now worth millions.

Yours ever,

RM

Dad proffers a bit of family history from the Branston Pickle and Baked Bean side of the family.

20 April

Dear Lupin,

Many thanks for the card. Colonel Burnaby, a relation of Freddy's, commanded the Blues and was a remarkable character. He was a famous traveller in the Middle East, fought in various wars and was eventually speared by a fuzzy-wuzzy in the Sudan. He was immensely strong and was liable to enter a room with a pony under each arm! There was quite a good book about him by a man I knew called Alexander.

Our trip to Devon was a failure. We both had 'flu-colds and were very crotchety and got on each other's nerves. I was rude and ill-tempered, while Nidnod would discuss stag-hunting with a bucolic waitress. Nidnod tried to get into conversation with a grumpy old man in a pub. He thought she was trying to pick him up and turned his back on her and walked out!

Otto behaved badly and ensured insomnia. I had a tiresome visit to the Royal Berks: that Iraqi Dr is useless. Poor Hot Hand Henry has lost his job and of course there are tears and grief down in Devonshire.

Richard McLaren was mugged in London and got his nose broken.

Icy cold here: by and large everything very depressing. Old age is vile and if I could afford it, which I can't, I'd go into a home and await the arrival of good old Mons.

Lunch with Caroline Blackwell (now Wells) tomorrow. Cousin John rang up about a funeral but could not remember whose it was.

Your affec. father,

D

Life goes on Chez Mortimer and on holiday in Devon. Dad's health is in decline.

The Miller's House
18 October

Dear Lupin,

Thank you so much for your help over the picture. I think the price was a fair one. When Christie's pay me, I will send you a small memento of the occasion.

I had a letter yesterday from Mr Grange of Dreweatt-Neate who did (free) a valuation of this house. His estimate was £375–£400,000. This means that Nidnod will have quite a valuable little property when I kick the bucket. Keith has an appalling cold and is unable to work in the garden.

Yours ever,

D

Few things give more pleasure to my father than whipping a painting off the wall, generally without my mother's knowledge or consent, and then flogging it for a tidy sum.

1990

The Miller's House
20 February

Dear Lupin,

Thank you so much for driving the Miller's House wrinkles up to London. Greatly appreciated. It was a fine service and Nidnod was clearly much moved. At lunch at the Turf Club I sat next to a man called Lambton who mentally is about 13/6d in the £. I wonder if he is related to Lucinda Lambton who does those bizarre programmes on TV. I don't much like Louise's dog. I think he may prove to be fierce.

Yours ever
RM

Lunches and family celebrations at the Turf Club were a constant for as long as I can remember. Grace, the legendary hall porter, once (with a wry look of amusement) gave my mother a leg up into the tractor unit of an articulated lorry I was driving. On another occasion I found my mother outside in animated discussion with a traffic warden explaining the reason why the parking ticket he had just issued should be voided: 'But, my dear man, I was once engaged to the Minister of Transport.'

25 October

Dear Lupin,

Thank you so much for your help over the picture. I enclose a small token of gratitude from Nidnod and myself.

David Reid-Scott and his new wife lunched here on Sunday. She is very attractive and intelligent as well.

Jane is very touchy over her sons. She did not like something I said and exploded, using language barely permissible in the Corporals' Mess and not exactly suitable in respect of her father. If she does not watch it, these boys will grow up a couple of softies churning out inferior poetry. Frankly I'd prefer them to get their House Colours.

I hope that you are enjoying Ealing. Perhaps one day you'll defend Nidnod on a speeding charge – I'm not well-versed in the law. Just after the war I was President of several Court Martials. There was mild trouble when I let a man off because his Commanding Officer was obviously a château-bottled shit.

Yours,
RFM

P.S. While on this subject, just after the war there was a corporal under my command at Wellington Barracks who undoubtedly murdered a homo artist in the Cromwell Road by bashing his head with an army boot. Proof, though, was unobtainable.

Aldershot was a great place for murders as people with bizarre tastes used to come down from London and pick up soldiers who frequently beat them up and robbed them.

There was a boy called Peel at Eton with me who went off his onion later and sawed the head off his ever-loving wife. He was very odd when the moon was full. I subsequently met him at Broadmoor where apparently he could be terrifying when he had one of his little moods. The only woman I recollect at Broadmoor was an ancient dame who years previously had distributed poisoned sweets to children at Brighton.

The nastiest man I ever met was a huge, hideous, immensely powerful Gestapo man who was confined before trial at Kensington Palace Gardens, where we supplied the guard. It gave me chills just to look at him.

Kensington P.G. was not very secure so he was removed to a compound at Kempton Park alleged to be escape-proof. He got out within twenty-four hours but was luckily recaptured – he was seen by the steward from the local golf-club and eventually hanged. He had murdered several of the RAF officers who escaped from the camp at Sagan.

Woe betide anyone who even mildly criticizes my sister's sons. To be fair, my dear mother is equally protective. As my dad would point out in exasperation when, yet again, my mother rushed to my defence in the face of the indefensible, 'A boy's best friend is his mother.' I have returned to school aged, thirty-eight, to study law.

1991

Dear Lupin,

So sorry you're having a rotten time and I sympathise: I know a lot about ill-health. Your mother loathes Dr Yates which is embarrassing for me as I rather like him, although I do not hold a lofty opinion of his medical skill. Still, one does not expect much from rural GPs except something from the 1897 Edition of Blacks Medical Dictionary.

GPs like the Yateley pair are very rare indeed. Some of our London ones were pretty bizarre. Can I help you over £.s.d? To help you in Criminal Law read books about great criminal lawyers like Marshall Hall, Carson, Patrick Hastings, Norman Birkett.

Lunching with Gaselees today.

All the best,

D

Both Dad and I have health problems. I am enjoying studying law at Ealing Polytechnic. One interest we share other than comedies such as Carry On films and On The Buses are classic British murder cases and great criminal lawyers. Edward Marshall Hall is a hero for both of us.

Very sadly this is the last correspondence from my father. He dies a few months later on 27 November 1991. At a thanks-giving service for his life I give a short address which includes the following rhyme by Harry Graham:

My son, Augustus, in the street, one day,
Was feeling quite exceptionally merry,
A stranger asked him; 'Can you show me, pray
The quickest way to Brompton Cemetery?'
'The quickest way? You bet I can,' said Gus,
And pushed the fellow underneath a bus.
Whatever people say about my son,
He does enjoy his little bit of fun.

Charlie Mortimer

Born 1952.

Educated: Wellesley House, Broadstairs, Eton and Davies Crammer. Left education 1969.

Career history includes: spell in the Coldstream Guards, vintage car restorer, proprietor of mobile discotheque, paint and cement salesman, agricultural labourer, construction labourer, painter and decorator, estate agent, property developer, oil rig roughneck, pop group manager, second-hand car and Unimog salesman, mechanic in Africa, maker of backgammon boards, scrap-metal dealer, Heavy Goods Vehicle Class 1 driver, including driving articulated trucks to Poland in support of Solidarnosc (1981–4), antiques dealer, manufacturer of boxer shorts, law student and financial and legal advisor (unofficial).

Since 1988: Director of Carlton Hobbs Ltd (antiques business) 1988–1993.

Director of John Hobbs Ltd (antiques business) 1994–2001.

Director of Simon Finch Rare Books Ltd (1996–2005).

Columnist 'Dr Mortimer's Observations', *Zembla* Magazine.

Currently 'middle-aged, middle-class spiv' (mostly retired).